CORRIS

A Narrow Gauge Portrait

By

John Scott Morgan

IRWELL PRESS

'Last Train Up'– the arrival of the last train at Aberllefenni, by Eric Bottomley.

Eric Bottomley

ISBN 1 871608 18 X

ACKNOWLEDGEMENTS

My first delvings into the Corris and its wooded valley began back in the 1970s, in the early years of the Corris Railway Society. *The Corris Railway Company*, a slim volume, appeared in 1977 as a consequence and this new work is the outcome of further investigation, and the acquisition of much new information, since then. For help, encouragement and assistance over all this time I would like to make grateful acknowledgement to many individuals and organisations, in no particular order of precedence .... W.H.A Edwards, Paul Braithwaite, The Talylln Railway, C.C.Green, W.A.Camwell, the LCGB, the LPC (Ian Allan), Dave Brewer, LGRP, H.C.Casserley, the RCTS, the HMRS, *Railway Magazine, Narrow Gauge Times, NGRS Magazine, Industrial Railways Journal,* National Library of Wales, National Museum of Wales, J. Jarvis, Don Boreham, Corris Railway Society, H.Smith, Nick Harden, Eric Bottomley, Victor Pearce, and a special thanks to Mrs Briwnant-Jones and to Gwyn Briwnant-Jones.
In this account I have drawn to a considerable degree upon contemporary reports, minutes and documents, to catch some of the atmosphere of Dix's fiefdom in the Dulas. I have not sought to 'correct' any of these period quotes for spelling, even where nineteenth century grapplings with Welsh lead to variations within the same paragraph. The Board of Trade, I'm sure, would have regarded any attempt at accurate rendition mildly eccentric, or even subversive; it serves to catch some of the air of Major Marandin's increasingly grumpy trips to the 'toy railway', and should offend nobody.

Published by

Irwell Press

3 Durley Avenue, Pinner, Middlesex, HA5 1JQ.

Printed by Amadeus Press, Huddersfield

'A trip to the lake' (see later) beckons outside Corris station. Rock in one form or another effectively fashioned life in the Dulas; much of the local economy depended on it, and looming up in bulk it pressed closely the fields and villages – even the graveyards.

Chapter One
Before the Railway;
Chapel and School, Wood and Barn

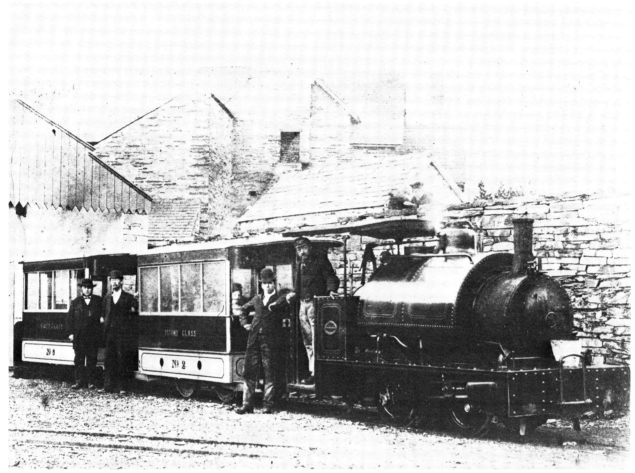

Aberllefenni-bound train at Corris in 1880. The 0-4-0ST, one of the trio recently supplied, is as yet unmodified to the 0-4-2 arrangement. The bouncing motion of the little tank, married to the short wheel base rigid 4-wheel 'tram cars' and the eccentric curves of the Corris permanent way, must have made for an undignified progress. 'That the Corris engines are often attributed to the Falcon Company is probably due to the plates which the engines carried in later years,' S.H.P. Higgins reveals in Railways in 1949. The actual builders, Hughes, had gone into liquidation in 1881 and the engines were rebuilt by its successors at the Falcon Works between 1895 and 1900. The plates would date from that period.

LGRP

The village of Corris lies five miles north of Machynlleth, at the head of a narrow winding valley where the River Dulas is joined by the Deri, flowing down from Corris Upper. Little is known of the early history of the area, though according to the *Cambrian Register* of 1795 the name Corris comes down from 'Corus'. There are those who would derive the name from the word Cor-is, Cor meaning path. 'Below path' would refer to the numerous sheep tracks and paths along the hills and mountain slopes.

There is perhaps an alternative to this, in that a party of monks from Llanbadarn, near Aberystwyth, led by St. Padarn, passed this way in 576 AD; it is believed that the Saint left a monk named Corus behind, when he and his followers moved on further north. Certainly the name Ffynnon Badarn Farm near Aberllefenni seems to point to this.

The Corris area survived largely upon sheep rearing, with cottage industries such as spinning, glove making and mason-work to back up the main economy. This and the general way of life changed completely when the slate industry established

itself from the 1790s to the 1850s. In the 1820s an average family in this remote district would probably have been involved with shepherding or spinning as a main occupation while others of the family would engage in part time work of a seasonal nature. This might include the collecting of lichen from the rocks and trees, to sell at 1½d a pound for dye making or the gathering of local ferns for burning; the ash was used in the soap and glass industries. Very often a large family would derive a weekly income of ten or twelve shillings from all these diverse local activities.

One other way for locals to eke a living was domestic service, which usually meant going far away from the district, seldom to return. Whichever way you look at the last century, especially in the first fifty years, life was hard and very often miserable.

There is one other occupation I have not mentioned, *wool washing* or *pandying*, common to the Corris and Machynlleth district. Very often a farm would have a small outhouse set aside in order to make some extra money from wool washing,

The 'two bridges' outside Corris. The train is interesting for the transitional nature of the stock – two early four wheel cars and a converted bogie vehicle. The last part of the nineteenth century on the Corris were the years of 'greatness' and Dix in one of his many communications with the Board of Trade was moved to pass on an item from the Oswestry & Border Counties Advertiser of 6th November 1889. It lies yellowing in the Public Record Office files today: 'Increasing popularity of the Corris Railway – We are informed that the Corris Railway Co. have carried over thirty thousand tourists this season, and over two thousand passengers were carried by the coaches plying between Corris and Machynlleth.'

for Welsh cloth. This was exported from local points like Aberdovey and Borth, to Europe and even as far away as America. Quite apart from this boat building thrived along the Dovey estuary, at Derwenlas to the west of Machynlleth. Many of the fine schooners built there plied the seven seas with Welsh slate, which was much in demand during the latter 1900s.

In 1888 there were sixty four farms in the area, which changed in the next fifty years as smallholdings were swallowed up and made into larger farms. Latterly, after 1914, the Forestry Commission took possession of the former grazing, turning it over to trees.

The land was poor and for hill farmers especially it was hard to make a living. For all this, there seemed to be a breed of hardy people in the district, maintaining small holdings well into the latter part of the 19th century. It was during this period, before the slate industry had made its mark, that much was achieved to mould the area and its place in Welsh history. Religious life had reached a low ebb at the end of the 1800s, with locals organising 'sports games and sales of various goods' (shock) after morning service. At that time, there was only one church in the parish, at Talyllyn. This was to change over the next thirty years, especially after the Methodist Revival. A new sexton, one Richard Anthony, arrived in the early 19th century and the unholy fun and games came to an end when he 'put a stop to them.' In the first decades after 1900 a number of Non Conforming chapels were built, a direct threat to the Anglican Church which had no places of worship in the Corris area. It was Lord Londonderry who made funds available to build Trinity Church at Corris in 1861, to save the local Anglicans from having to go all the way to Talyllyn to worship. In the late 19th century a new corrugated iron Anglican Church was built at Upper Corris; known locally as 'Eglwys Zinc' it served the area for many years before services began at

Esgairgeiliog. 'Eglwys Zinc' went out of use, finally becoming a community centre in the 1960s.

Methodists had come to the area late in the 1800s, when services were held at a house named Tyn Yr Wdin, in Upper Corris. There was some antagonism towards the Methodists at first and rowdies would often try to disrupt services. However, as time went by the movement grew and a large number of chapels and meeting houses were established. It was in fact an offence at the time for Methodists to hold services, punishable by a fine of £100 or exile, this being one penalty of the Conventicle Act – the heinous offence of 'preaching without a licence'. After the Revival of 1819 the number of local Methodists rose to over 70; in 1813 Dafydd Wmffra had given them some land near Aber Corris where they built a chapel called Rehoboth. A second chapel was built in 1834 and later in 1846 land was given for a cemetery on the hillside above. By 1869 there was need for a third chapel in the area; this was built but on February 19th 1922 floods swept most of it away. A new enlarged building now stands on safer ground on the Aberllefenni Road, to the design of Sir Howell J. Williams, architect of the Corris Institute.

The Methodist movement was also progressing in the Upper Corris area, where Sunday schools and other church activities were taking place. Also a number of land plots were purchased, to enlarge existing buildings, though most of these schemes did not take place, as the population declined after World War One. Meetings and services were also held in the Aberllefenni area in private houses and in 1874 a chapel was built on the road from Corris known as Capel Y Methodistiaid. There was also a chapel near Ratgoed Quarry with a capacity of 100, opened in 1871, but congregations were always small and most people went to chapel in Aberllefenni. The Wesleyans had first come to the area in 1802, early meetings taking place in the hamlet of Maes Y Gorwyr. In the Dulas valley it

2

appears that regular prayer meetings were held in members' houses, and a Sunday school was started at Cwmeiddaw in 1804. The first moves were made to build a chapel, probably close to where Moriah Wesleyan chapel now stands. The *Little Chapel,* as it was called locally, was used until 1838, when the membership had declined to only six. As the nineteenth century progressed more chapels and meeting houses came into being, a notable one being Carmel, built by the main road at Lower Corris in 1838. There was so much enthusiasm for services that meetings were held there before the windows or internal decor were complete.

The Wesleyans were very much involved with the Temperance Movement and The Band of Hope (the 'Cold Water Army'); so much so that Carmel chapel would not allow any preacher involved in its activities to drink, even in moderation. This made for a serious dispute with higher authority, in Machynlleth no less, which would not allow any preacher or lay preacher to attend Carmel until the ban was lifted in 1852. The chapel was enlarged but the greatest change was to come in 1859, with the Revival which swept the area. After two months most if not all the local inns were empty (apparently) as the population attended services, both on Sundays and each evening. There were even meetings during meal breaks in the quarries. By 1816 the first small schools for local children were being established, mostly held in private dwellings. The quarrymen were responsible for setting up the first adult education in the area, in the form of workers groups which met in the cabins at lunchtime. Great debates on religious and literary matters would take place. After 1870 each village along the valley had its own school and most of the small local groups ceased.

There are those who say that the slate industry probably started in the district around 1500, though this would only be surface extraction, by a small number of men working on the open cast principle. The first working proper did not start to function in the area until 1810, the Aberllefenni Quarry. From 1810 to 1850 quarries were opened up in the valley from Llwyngwern to Ratgoed and Upper Corris. The population grew from 350 in 1810 to over 2,000 in 1868, a level of increase spurred on by the growth of the slate industry and continuing until production peaked in the early 1900s.

Sadly all industry has a negative as well as a positive side, and the large scale mining and quarrying over 150 years has left some ugly scars on the local landscape. Time and tide and so the course of history was moving on. Local prosperity moved with it, towards an uncertain future, though one in which local people could at least hope for improvement in their lives, in the remote valley of the Dulas. It was now the dawn of a new era, when crude road transport would give way to a more effective and efficient medium – the railway. Horse operated at first, later would come the *terrible hissing steed,* rousing this place of horse track, chapel, barn and wood.

The formidable Cold Water Army, on one of its regular punitive sallies into the Dulas.

'Esgairgeiliog Pass' looking towards Corris, c. 1900. The peculiar troughing carries the water supply for machinery at the local quarry.
Brian Hilton Collection

Chapter Two
Early Times;
Troubles with the Board of Trade

A remote wooded cleft deep in central Wales, wealth was to be won from the Dulas Valley in the unlikely form of a blue-black fissile rock – slate. The value of this ancient rock in building and monumental work and its uniquely fine suitability for roofing, had long been recognised and a quarrying and mining industry of prodigious proportions grew up in the tract of hill country from mid to north Wales and Snowdonia. 'Slate' by broadest definition is found widely in Britain in the geologically older areas but it varies enormously in its ease of working; nowhere is the best stuff found in such abundance and quality as North Wales.

It is a rock of great ancientness, owing its origins to the fine mud and silt detritus of deep sea troughs, cascading gently to the sea bottom hundreds of millions of years ago. In the succeeding, yawning, ages of time it was first buried deep under the weight of its own sediments, then drawn within the earth by subsidence, to be heated and contorted miles below, finally revealed again at the surface by faulting and rock movements on a vast scale. By this time it is wholly altered, the original soft black mud now a hard smooth and resistant slab-like rock. It characteristically splits (or 'cleaves') along parallel surfaces; this is the 'slate' quality that is so prized, imparted by the heating and pressure it has endured over aeons. The more precisely 'baked' the slate is and the finer and more even the original grain size of it as an earlier mud, the better its facility for splitting. Slate has thus been wholly altered by geological process from its original condition – it is hence termed a 'metamorphic' (that is, a rock *changed in form*), in contrast say to a 'volcanic' (like lava) or a 'sedimentary' rock (sandstone for instance). Slow and prolonged baking then, a process which, crucially, stopped short of melting, in the oven of the earth over millions of years, imparted the commercially desirable qualities now made available in a few locations in Wales. In the Dulas Valley slate of varying quality could be won, suited to different purposes – there were for instance beds of a particularly fine rock, making for excellent insulating properties in heavy electrical engineering applications, and for high quality monumental work.

Tradition holds that the earliest workings took place even in Roman times and over the centuries since, various small open pits were intermittently worked for local needs. The stirring growth of industrialisation way beyond the woods and hills of the Dulas demanded more cut and slab slate than could be handled in the old way – lone horses picking their way down the valley with crude sledges, along rough hewn paths. The sledges were got to Machynlleth and thence onto Quay Ward on the River Dovey, some three miles further westwards. From here it took to the sea, for a market that was not simply to be confined to Britain but was worldwide.

There were obvious limitations to this inching, laboured progress and the quarry owners, impatient of the uncertain mountain paths, determined upon a properly engineered tramroad. This would link the workings to the north, at Ratgoed, Aberllefenni and the new Upper Corris seams to Machynlleth, and thence Quay Ward, replicating in effect the earlier 'natural' route but with all the easements of grade a

proper construction could bring. The inspiration apparently flowed from the example of the Festiniog Railway and an assortment of tramways throughout many parts of the Welsh hills. The resulting survey, conducted by a Thomas Nicholls, manifested itself as *The Corris, Machynlleth and River Dovey Tramroad* of 1850. In name unwieldy and over-grand, the project remained dormant until the eventual passing of a Parliamentary Act in 1858.

The tramroad opened to traffic as far as Machynlleth on 1st April 1859 at a gauge of 2ft 3ins, using horses. The Act embodied a number of restrictions, the most notable being a prohibition on the use of steam locomotion. These were considered inappropriate for such tramways – understandable when one observes the lurching nature of the permanent way, (though its quality was much praised in latter years) even when upgraded for steam working. The earliest contemporary description of the line comes from an unlikely source, the French Engineer, M.E.Vignes. He was principally concerned with the Festiniog and its working but on the Corris, in his *Étude Technique sur le Chemin de Fer de Festiniog et quelques autres Chemins de Fer a voieétroite de l'angleterre*, he had much to say:

The Corris was first incorporated by an Act of 15 & 16, Victoria, Cap 166, on 1st July 1852, under the name of the Corris, Machynlleth and River Dovey Tramroad Company. The Company, having allowed the powers conferred on it to lapse without having completed its lines, obtained an extension under an Act of 1858. These two Acts authorised it to build a railway or tramroad between the slate quarries at Aberllefenny in the parish of Tal-y-Llyn, County of Merioneth, and Machynlleth, a locality situated on the River Dovey. The length of this line was to be about 24 km (15 miles).

The track was laid in fairly ancient fashion, light 15lb bridge rail on wooden sleepers, with dog spikes securing rails to wooden ties. Loaded wagons were worked by gravity, presumably, on the steeper inclines from the quarry faces themselves, and down the valley, with horses hauling them on the more or less level stretches on to Machynlleth, Derwenlas and the Dovey. The engineer 'was Arthur Causton of Gloucester', who estimated the costs of construction at £15,000.

So unsuited was the track, however, that steam locomotives were prohibited, the Act even containing a punitive clause, giving the Board of Trade authority to fine the company £100 a day (a greater sum possibly than the entire daily economy of the valley and beyond) should it dare to make use of steam. Proper 40lb flat bottom rail was to be used if locomotives were to be contemplated; the conversion of the Festiniog to the new fangled working in 1863 had however demonstrated its suitability and in the same year the standard gauge had opened to Machynlleth from the east – the Newtown & Machynlleth Railway – in January. In July the Aberystwyth and Welsh Coast Railway had forged onwards to the west, crossing over the Corris, Machynlleth and River Dovey Tramroad immediately west of Machynlleth station and on the level,

TAL-Y-LLYN LAKE AND CADER IDRIS , CORRIS RAILWAY. 8.

further down the valley at Quay Ward.

It was a revolutionary time for the valley quarries. There was now a proper link to the outside world, removing the risky business of a sea journey; better still bigger and more immediate markets beckoned. The whole operation of the lines, it was clear, required upgrading; the standard gauge link at Machynlleth with the (from 1864) Cambrian Railways, promised a burgeoning traffic which the tramroad's horses had little prospect of satisfying. By a further Act of 1864 the conversion of the line to steam operation, the formal abandonment of its stretch beyond Machynlleth and the adoption of the name Corris Railway was authorised. Vignes again:

In 1864 the Company was incorporated by a new Act (27 & 28, Victoria, Chap. 225, of 25th July 1864), under the name of the Corris Railway Company ... This latest Act has moreover permitted the Company to use locomotives to work the line, which had been forbidden by the previous Acts.

Despite the advances of its contemporaries, the Festiniog and the Talyllyn, the newly constituted Corris languished, or at least seemed content with matters much as they had been through the 1860s and 1870s. Vignes' visits to the narrow gauge lines of Wales took place in the autumn of 1877 and his observations of the Corris (published in 1878) though limited, are illuminating – authorised capital under the 1852 Act had been £16,000 and under the 1864 Act a further maximum of £32,000 had been allowed. By Vignes' visit only £20,000 had been taken up. 'Information about the construction of this little line is lacking', he declares, and rolling stock was limited to 'but a small number of slate wagons and a small number of open wagons recently used for carrying passengers ... haulage is by horses and the rolling stock is supplied by the slate companies or by the businesses which use the line. The transformation of the Corris Railway into a locomotive hauled line, although authorized by the Act of 1864, has so far not taken place ... the Corris is still only a sort of tramway like the Festiniog Railway was before 1864. Its traffic however has increased somewhat over the past few years, and passenger traffic began in 1874. [The line was, then, carrying passengers at this early time, by 1860 in fact, though presumably these would, perforce, have travelled on an irregular and unofficial basis] ... this service is still very primitive and is performed by open horse drawn wagons ...'

In the year of Vignes' commentary an extraordinary change occurred in the constitution of The Corris when, 'lock stock and barrel' it passed into the hands of the *Imperial Tramways Company*. The simple contrast in names augured something of a shake-up for the plodding horseway of the Dulas Valley and subsequent events lived up (well, a bit at least) to the rather broader horizons implicit in the title of the new parent company.

The first General Manager, the mercurial Mr J.R. Dix, was installed, for the more obscure the line, the more energetic and publicity-minded the General Manager needed to be, it seems. Conacher, a contemporary of Dix on the neighbouring Cambrian for a time, was a good example. Put in charge of the shambling Isle of Wight Central, he achieved interviews in the railway press on a par with the LNWR and other giants. He and Dix in many ways were precise contemporaries.

A transhipment wharf had been built at Machynlleth, by 1866, and by the time of Imperial Tramway's accession very little traffic was leaving by sea on the old tram extension west from Machynlleth to Quay Ward, closed in 1878.

The Corris had finally got around to ordering steam locomotives, a trio suitably numbered 1, 2 and 3 and built by Hughes Ltd at the Falcon Works, Loughborough in 1878. All were delivered in November, subsequently to be variously rebuilt (see later captions) and were joined by a further example from Kerr Stuart, No.4, years later in 1921. With the Board of Trade strictures very much in mind the summer of 1878 was occupied with replacement of the old wrought iron bridge rail by 40lb flat bottom, from Aberllefenni through Corris to Machynlleth. The original bridge rail to Ratgoed and Upper Corris was left, for the undemanding needs of horse working, until closure in 1948.

Lewis Cozens wrote with great originality of the Corris, and it is through his pioneering efforts that a complete book should be devoted to it, *The Corris Railway*, in 1949, a time when railway books were few and far between. It was reprinted by the Corris Railway Society in 1972, and perhaps its most pleasing features (among many) are the fruits of Cozens' trawlings in the local press; this is a snippet found by him in the *Aberystwyth Observer* of 23rd November 1878: *The origin of the tramway must be attributed to the indefatigable exertions of Mr. Thomas Smith Nicholls, who made a survey of it in the year 1850. Such a mad scheme was pooh-poohed at the time, but it proved a reality, and the first train passed over the Dovey river to Machynlleth on the 1st April 1859...*

And more ... *22nd June 1878. Corris Tramway ... used for conveying slates, slabs and even passengers from Corris slate districts, is to have locomotives put on as soon as arrangements are complete. This is another step in the right direction and doubtless will bring more 'fish to the net' to benefit the trade of the town ...*

... 9th November 1878. Some splendid carriages have arrived at Machynlleth for the Corris and Machynlleth Railway Company. They are constructed upon the principle of the road tramway carriages, with doors and breaks at both ends. They weigh about a ton each and are very handsome: the first class cushions are covered with green plush. They were manufactured at Hughes' Locomotive and Tramway Engine Works, Loughborough. They are at present drawn by two horses, but ultimately a locomotive will be attached when the road is complete and passed by the Government Inspector.

There then followed a period of spirited infighting in the Dulas Valley, for the energetic Dix and his company with its background of passenger transport in towns was resolved upon a passenger service for his line, beyond the intermittent (and covert) one so far attempted. Cozens has culled some splendid extracts from *The Aberystwyth Observer* which had enthusiastically greeted the arrival of the locomotives ('it will bring more fish to the net' 'some splendid carriages etc') and Cozens quotes from the issue of 9th November 1878 ...

... the new carriages recently placed on the Corris Tramway prove a boon this severe weather to the number of passengers who patronise it, and the speed is very much accelerated by the use of two horses instead of one. The station is nearing completion: it is 66ft long, with a booking office at the village end, glass roof and platform under cover. The goods department is a short distance from the village in close proximity to the turnpike road near the Braichgoch Hotel. The iron horse is expected to arrive shortly. It will be put into requisition for the conveyance of slates, goods, etc., but not for passenger traffic until the line has passed the Government Inspector.

The quarry owners were less than happy at the prospect of a passenger service and apparently regarded such nonsense as an erosion, which could only worsen, of the service available to them. The company was debarred from carrying passengers and had thus in any event to seek Parliamentary sanction. This was opposed by the various quarry owners who had grown accustomed to using the tramway much as they pleased, neglecting to pay in plenty of instances. A proper passenger service, with all the regulation and overseeing thereby

Train over the Dovey, on the original trestle bridge. It deteriorated of course and Dix was naturally charged with the task of renewal. At first, in the autumn of 1902, the bridge had merely been regarded as 'defective' and 'certain repairs' were ordered to be 'carried out forthwith'. It was 1905 before the need to reconstruct the bridge became apparent. Dix obtained tenders in May 1906, £412 for the ironwork and £465 for the coffer dams, and 'it was agreed that the work of rebuilding the bridge should be carried out by the Company, under the supervision of the Managing Director.'

Brian Hilton Collection

implied, was viewed with some distaste.

The new locomotives were put to hauling slate and goods only, an attempt at a Bill for allowing passenger services failing through the owners' objections in 1879. This was not well received locally and a Bill the following year, 1880, did meet with success, though various delays meant the Board of Trade Inspection, necessary for opening to passengers, could not be made for another couple of years. The story is largely contained in the Board of Trade record, voluminous out of all proportion to the size of the Corris and increasingly exasperated in tone. The saga begins with one Morris Thomas, a druggist living in Corris, writing to The Rt. Hon. J. Chamberlain MP, on July 13th 1880:

Sir, I beg respectfully to bring under your notice the present state of the Corris Railway, the Bill of which is understood to have just received the Royal Assent.

It is stated by the officials employed in the construction of the railway that it is now ready for Government inspection. It is very probable that many alterations and additions have to be made to complete the line for passenger traffic, but I wish to point out what I believe is a necessity for the public safety, viz, the construction of a high wall between the turnpike road and the railway. The latter runs as close as 2ft to the other for a distance of about four miles, and there is only a wire fence in some parts and a bare hedge for six months in the year in other parts to hide it from view on the turnpike road. The railway traffic will therefore be so open to the turnpike road that with the many sharp curves on the line it must be highly dangerous to the gentry, the farmers and public generally travelling with horses on the turnpike road.

Trusting you will deem the above worthy of your consideration I remain, etc.'

'We might send a copy to the Company' is the only comment from the (obviously less than impressed) Board of Trade.

The Corris Secretary in defence of the company's activities declared:

It is not and never has been the slightest intention of opening the line for passenger traffic until it has been duly passed by the Board of Trade. Under the powers granted by the Act of 1864 steam has been used for conveyance of the goods traffic on this line since the commencement of 1878 without complaint of any kind being made.

The Board of Trade nonetheless pondered this, noting that under some sort of regulation (the Board itself seemed unclear as to which) screens could be required on turnpike roads. A Henry Sewell, in what appears to have been a concerted campaign, wrote in July 1880...

Sir, I beg to bring the following circumstances under the consideration of the Board of Trade. I live at Llangwern, [sic] a residence which I rent from the Marquis of Londonderry about three miles from the town of Machynlleth whence I and my family frequently drive. At a distance of some 300 yards from the town we have to cross the Corris tramway on a level crossing at which there is no person in charge. If the Corris tramway is allowed to carry passengers by steam we shall be in danger of being run over in crossing the line as a train coming from Corris can only be seen a few yards off. I have not lived long in the neighbourhood but I understand that the crossing has existed ever since the tramway has been made about twenty years ago. There was no danger in using the crossing until the recent introduction of steam for working the line which was previously worked by horsepower.

A train at Machynlleth about 1903. This is the old station, primitive even by Corris standards; in June 1903 Dix prevailed upon the Board to effect its replacement: 'The Managing Director reported as to the necessity for rebuilding Machynlleth station and that he had given instructions for the work to be proceeded with. His action in the matter was approved.'

National Railway of Wales

May I also call particular attention to the extreme danger to the public in driving along the turnpike road which runs parallel with and close to the tramway for a distance of about four miles, about two miles each way from the above crossing. I understand that although Parliament has in the present session authorised the use of steam for the conveyance of passengers it is still necessary for the company to have the tramway inspected under the direction of the Board of Trade and any object in now writing is to point out the extreme importance to the public travelling along the turnpike road that provision be made against accidents from the use of the locomotives.

Yet another protagonist assailed the Board at this time, a Mr. John Evans of the Lion Hotel, Machynlleth, but though there is no copy of his letter the BoT reply runs simply: 'Your comments will be referred to the Officer who may be appointed to inspect the railway.' This turned out to be Major Marindin, whose Report is dated 7th October 1880:

This single line was originally constructed as a mineral line only under the Corris Machynlleth and River Dovey Tramway Act of 1858. Under the Corris Railway Act 1880, a length of 5 miles 0.25 chains has been altered and improved for passenger traffic, the speed being under this Act limited to 15 miles an hour. It commences in the goods yard of the Cambrian station ... and the portion submitted for inspection terminates at Corris. It is intended to work with one engine in steam only and the only passenger traffic expected is that of the slate quarry villages. No land has been purchased for an additional line of rails. The gauge is 2ft 3ins and the width between the rails where double at the passing places is 5ft. The rails are of Vignoles pattern weighing 44lbs per yard and generally in 24ft lengths. They are fastened by dog spikes to cross sleepers 4ft 4ins long and 8ft 4¾ ins laid 3ft apart. There are clip bolts with facing washers at each joint and at the centre of each rail. The joints are fished. The ballast is broken slate and earth and river gravel, the fencing is of wire fencing, stone walls and hedges.

The line rises the whole way from Machynlleth to Corris, the steepest gradient being 1 in 35, throughout in some places upon curves with as small a radius as two chains. The two chain curves are checked. There are stations at Machynlleth, Pandy, ['later Llwyngwern'] Esgairgeiliog and Corris. The intermediate stations have passing places, where one line only has been signalled for use. Besides the sidings at all the stations except Pandy there is a manual line junction and engine shed sidings at Maespoeth. There are no over bridges, there is a timber viaduct across the River Dovey and five other bridges over streams, three of which have stone arches and two have stone abutments with timber superstructures. There are two culverts.

The arch of one bridge requires repair but otherwise these works which were constructed when the line was first made are in good order. There is only one level crossing of a public road and this is provided with proper gates and lodge and signals. The rolling stock consists of three four wheeled saddle tank engines with 2ft 6ins wheels, 4ft wheelbase and a weight of six tons. They were built by Hughes of Loughborough and motions are not balanced. There are four first class and six second class carriages with four wheels and 3ft 8ins wheelbase having end doors and no windows at the side which can be opened. Each carriage has a break. There is a low platform at Corris but none at the other stations. The accommodation at Machynlleth consists of a bare shed without any proper approach and with no urinals or conveniences. At the intermediate stations the only building is the signal hut. At Corris

there is a covered shed and urinal but no separate accommodation for ladies. Throughout the line walls, banks, houses, trees, signal posts and telegraph poles are, in a great number of places, indeed generally, between one foot and 6 inches of the side of the carriages and engine. The fencing wants additions at Machynlleth and a few other places but generally is sufficient.

For these reasons I must report that in consequence of the incompleteness of the works this line cannot be opened to passenger traffic without danger to the public using the same. It is however altogether more of the nature of a steam tramway than a railway, the authorised speed being only three miles an hour more and the rolling stock of a similar character and before reporting as to the additional works which should be undertaken I submit that the question should be deferred for joint consideration of the inspecting officer.

Signed

Marandin (Major).

The Corris (not slow to spot a loophole) subsequently tried to get out of this by asking to be regarded as a tramway but after further inspections, in December 1880, the Board still could not recommend or sanction the opening, 'either as a railway or as a tramway'. The Board of Trade then had to issue a 'monthly postponement order', an administrative chore with which it soon lost patience. The miserable Corris was again approached, with firmness if not brevity, on 21st October 1881:

Dear Sir,

Would it not be as well for your Company to withdraw the second notice of opening, as requested in the concluding paragraph of the letter from this department of today's date covering the order for further postponing the opening of the Corris Railway? The suggestion is made in order to avoid the necessity of serving such orders from month to month until the railway is completed since when such is the case it will only be necessary for the Company to renew the second notice and the railway could then be re-inspected within ten days from the receipt thereof by this department.

The monthly notices had continued through 1881, though the Corris did as it was bidden, withdrawing the second notice of opening on 2nd November. In January 1882 a Mr. Kincaid, acting it would seem as Secretary to the Corris, agreed to 'get everything done.' On July 3rd 1882 he writes to the Board of Trade 'that the additions and alterations specified are now complete with one exception, viz; the curve at Coedwig Bridge where it is impossible from the position of the high road on one side and the river on the other to obtain a flatter curve than 4 chains, looking at the fact that the speed of trains on the railway is limited by Act of Parliament and the gauge is only 2ft 3ins I trust that the Board of Trade will not insist upon these requirements being carried out before issuing a licence for passenger traffic.'

Major Marandin re-inspected and was unimpressed, for opening again had to be postponed. By July 1882 postponements were once again being issued month by month. In October 1882 the Corris proposed to 're-apply to Parliament to authorise passenger traffic over the line ... before proceeding further I should like to know whether the Board of Trade has any objection to this being done. The reply was 'no' ... 'providing speed is mechanically limited to 12 m.p.h. and no curve is sanctioned with a less radius than 2 chains.'

Corris, resting in its hills around 1900, the tourist trade well under way even then. Beyond are the scars of the Braichgoch workings and the line itself (notice the signal post) threads across the middle of the picture. Corris station seems to be obscured but the line can be made out, disappearing off to the right, towards Garneddwen.

Brian Hilton Collection

In December 1882 the Board of Trade received a petition in favour of the Corris Railway being opened for traffic, though the document itself is missing from the Public Record. A further Bill 'to enable the Corris Railway Company to use their railways for passenger traffic and for other purposes' (i.e. to get away with tighter curves) followed, and on 21st June Fraser, by now the Corris Secretary, wrote to the Board of Trade asking for inspection – 'my directors are desirous of opening the railway for passenger traffic as soon as possible so as to secure a share of the summer excursion traffic and they will therefore be glad if you will appoint the earliest possible date for inspection of the line.' It was Major Marandin again and on 5th July 1883 we find him writing of the Corris again:

I have inspected the Corris Railway; the permanent way and other details of this single line remain as they were when I originally inspected it in 1880 but the curves have been altered and they are now laid in under the conditions of the Corris Railway Act 1883. The intermediate stations have been removed and there are now stations only at Machynlleth and Corris. There are two level crossings of public roads, one of which at the time of my first inspection was stated to be a private road, a notice to that effect being posted up. I can recommend that upon the receipt of a satisfactory undertaking as to the mode of working with one engine only in steam the opening of this single line for passenger traffic may be sanctioned. Phew!

On 26th October 1883 George Owen, who seems to have acted as Engineer to the Corris, writes to the company to declare that he sees no problem regarding 'new stations at Esgairgeiliog and Llwyngwern provided the proper waiting

sheds are erected and proper representation is made to the Board of Trade.'

On December 10th 1883 Colonel Gourley, one of the Corris Directors, writes to the Board of Trade and sends a drawing (see our copy) of the proposed stations at Esgairgeiliog and Llwyngwern: 'I now beg to hand you a sketch of the proposed station buildings. I also send you an extract from our Manager's letter: [this would be from Dix, who was usually lumbered with most jobs] I am sorry that I could not complete the enclosed sketch in time to send off last night. In addition to the sketch the Board of Trade will require positions of the proposed stations as follows:

Llwyngwern at 2 miles 21 chains 50 ell measured from Machynlleth, gradient 1 in 157, curve 21.52 chains to the left.

Esgairgeiliog at 3 miles 43 chains 50 ell measured from Machynlleth, gradient 1 in 187, curve 13.53 chains to the left.

Both stations will be on the right hand side of the line in going from Machynlleth to Corris.

The Board of Trade took note on the 11th October 1883, the reporting officer declaring 'I do not think there there is any necessity to oblige the Company to put in loops at these stations, the Company might therefore be informed that they may erect stations at these places without any platforms and without loops but that it will be necessary to provide the usual sanitary conveniences.'

The Corris write again on February 1884, to the Board of Trade. 'Two stations are now complete with the exception of painting and we would like them inspected.' Major Marindin trudged his way to the Dulas yet again and duly recommended the new stations in a Report of Thursday March 6th 1884.

The Corris was at last taking shape ...

12

No.4, 'the new engine', around 1924. This had been purchased in 1921 from Kerr Stuart & Co. (works No. 4047) and several accounts describe its name as 'Tattoo'. By 1926 it 'was the only engine in regular use as the other two are being reconstructed'. The old No.1 of the original trio had been withdrawn in 1920. The first carriage is Metropolitan No.7 (all differed in some detail or other), the second a rebuild from a pair of 'tram cars'. The third and last vehicle is 'the break'.

Real Photographs, Ian Allan

CADER IDRIS FROM CORRIS COACH ROAD, CORRIS RAILWAY. 11A.

The Corris area is dominated by the vast massif of Cader Idris, a sprawling and complex bulk of igneous and volcanic rocks, in marked contrast to the slate upon which the Dulas depended.

Brian Hilton Collection

Chapter Three
Interesting Times;
The Great Extension

Train at Aberllefenni in August 1930. This is No.3, with two Metropolitan coaches; the third is a clerestory (a rebuilt Falcon).

R.G. Jarvis

By December 1886 we find the Corris 'desirous of being relieved from the obligation to use the mechanical arrangement for limiting the speed of engines on their railway.' The Board of Trade learns that 'the arrangement in use gives considerable trouble by its constantly getting out of order', and further ... 'that it has not been considered necessary and it not used on other railways of a similar construction. In these current times the Board of Trade has advised sanctioning the mechanical arrangements being dispensed with, the condition as to the speed of 12 m.p.h. being observed.' So that was the end of any governing device; given the nature of working on the Corris it surely would have been been doomed in any event.

From opening in July 1883, all objections overcome and quarry owners in retreat (though the seeds of much cussedness and recalcitrance on their part had been sown), the line settled down to a routine; from August in the first year five trains a day each way were scheduled, timed at 25 or 30 minutes.

Perhaps the new passenger traffic was just as well, for the 1880s were not good for slate and one quarry, Abercwmeiddaw, was 'unable to fix a date for payment' of its three months account in 1885, no less than £99.19s. It was forced to pay cash from March 26th and afterwards experienced prolonged closure, though new workings were made at Ratgoed and Cymerau. The tale of the Corris from hereon is principally the ups and downs of business with occasional drama and tragedy. In 1885 the Abercorris Quarry Co. had several wagonloads confiscated in lieu of bad debts to the railway and was forced to close in November.

Someone was killed on the horse worked branch to Braichgoch Quarry. Kids had larked about with standing wagons and the Board of Trade subsequently ordered all wagons not in use to be secured to the rails, though the urgency of this stipulation is likely to have faded somewhat over the years.

The Braichgoch Quarry proved troublesome and a squabble over 'rights' broke out in 1887*. The operators were apparently still accustomed to take horse drawn wagons along the locomotive worked 'main line' more or less whenever they felt like it (!) and the Corris in time managed to dissuade them, drawing on the terms of its Act. The quarry manager in fact claimed use of the line for 2 hours in the morning and 2 hours in the afternoon but powers were unearthed in the 1880 Act to prohibit this. Llwyngwern and Esgairgeiliog became timetabled stops in the October 1886 timetable, instead of usual 'signal stops.'

The Corris was it seems a paternalistic and benign employer though like many Victorian concerns it could be highly litigious and was zealous in pursuit of its rights (or wrongs). The unfortunate Griffith Edwards fell foul of the Company in 1885; 'this man' the Directors heard 'had jumped from a train while running near Machynlleth and (here it gets bizarre) had 'recently wounded a sheep and driven it upon the Company's premises.' The Directors, plainly appalled, ordered that he 'be prosecuted for leaving the train and if possible for the other offence.' The hapless Edwards (was it a grudge? was he mad?) duly found himself in court in July 1885, to be fined 1 shilling and costs amounting to 30 shillings. Not content the Directors ordered 'that Bills be printed stating the offence and conviction and exhibited at the stations.' Thus publicly scourged, the wretch Edwards and his argument with the Corris fades from the Minutes. Perhaps he left the valley in shame, or was lauded a hero? The Directors doubtless would have seen him transported at the least. Failing, that is, a public hanging.

'All permanent way and buildings' were reported in good order in July 1885 and the 'resleepering of the Main Line' was proceeding apace, 800 out of the first 2000 large sleepers having been delivered and paid for (£40). The Dolgelley

Highway Board had been paid its annual £1 for the practice of working loaded Corris goods wagons over roads, for delivery to shops and so on, but passenger traffic was reported down, a disappointment over the corresponding month in 1884, figures due, it was said ...'to there having been an Eisteddfod and other attractions last July.'

The Director, Colonel Gourley, and an expert in such matters, paid a visit to Corris and presented recommendations to the Board in October 1885. These were accepted, that 'square creosoted sleepers should be used on the curves at the joints and middle of the rails and that a trial of galvanised and tar spikes should be made'.

Dix, the General Manager next wrote, for he was concerned about the less than impressive road approach 'from the Cambrian station to the Corris station at Machynlleth ... by putting a wall alongside the turnpike road and fencing in a footpath for which he had obtained permission from the Secretary and Engineer of the Cambrian ... cost would be about £30.' Dix knew his Board and like every good *apparatchik* allowed scope in the estimates for the Board to exercise its proper economising functions; 'it is desirable' announced the Directors 'to carry out the improvement ... if it can be effected for £15 to £20.'

There was an accident to a down train, the 4.25 pm, on 17th October 1885, three carriages and the break van having been 'thrown off the line' at Machynlleth by 'a platelayer acting as signal man'. 'The man has been dismissed' ends the account.

The first report of takings at Ffridd Gate 'at which the trains had stopped if required since October 2nd' was received on 20th November and had amounted to £3.0s.9d for the month. The Talyllyn enquired around this time regarding the availability of 'the spare engine' but the Board resolved not to let it go for less than 'the original cost, £700.' The company continued to be plagued by late payment from the quarries and the Directors were slightly put out to receive a letter of complaint with one long overdue cheque, bemoaning the 'pressing for payment.' At the end of November services were stopped with the line 3 feet under water at Machynlleth and the rain such that a landslip had occurred at Coedwig Curve.

The sad news came in December that the Company horse at Machynlleth had cut its foot; it 'was recovering' but better tidings came regarding the Abercorris account − £20 of their six month old debt of £56.9s.9d turned up (it was necessary to be grateful for small mercies) and the Secretary was instructed to pursue the balance.

Floods occurred again at Machynlleth on January 3rd 1886, this time 'to a depth of 3 and a half feet' and on threat of legal action the Abercorris coughed up a another £5 (!) with a further £15 promised ... 'during the week.'

There were enamelling works also in the Dulas Valley and in a case of biter bit the works at Esgairgeiliog had demanded £5 annual rental, on a bridge there 'communicating with the siding at the station'. Dix had offered a pound and proposed if it were not accepted simply 'to take up the points.' Dix wrote to Conacher of the Cambrian (see earlier) in February; destined to outshine him in mastery of publicity, he asked that photographs of Talyllyn Lake in Cambrian 1st class carriages should be altered. The Lake was described as 'near Towyn' and Dix, with little feel for the poetic romanticism the Victorians attached to such 'sights', felt this should be amended

---

*The Company had offered a rate of 2s per ton to the Braichgoch in May 1885, with a rebate of 1s per ton on any quantity in excess of 5000 tons over six months. 'Mr John Davies' wrote on April 27th, and at a quantity of 500 − 1000 tons per week was offered a rate of 1s or 1s 3d if the total fell below 500 tons. The Corris loved this sort of arrangement.

Train on the reconstructed Dovey Bridge. This was easily the principal engineering feature of the line, four girder spans over the Afon Dyfi; 240 feet long, the bridge also carried a footway.

(every bit helps) to read 'near Corris via Machynlleth.' The Directors approved the zeal and diligence of their General Manager but recommended him, hardly gently, 'to adopt a more conciliatory tone in his correspondence with the Cambrian.'

The new approach road to Machynlleth station was completed in February 1886 for some £20 and grim reports came from the Engineer working at the Coedwig curve. The slip on 28th November had not been the first apparently, for a retaining wall was considered necessary 'and that the road be kept well ballasted to prevent damage to the sleepers by the horses' feet.'

The fatal accident referred to earlier occurred on the Braichgoch branch on 31st May 1886, 'a lad, Joseph Hughes, letter carrier, and two children got onto an empty wagon at Upper Corris and set it in motion down the line, it had overturned at the quarry and one of the boys was killed, Hughes having his leg broken. The Coroner's Jury had recommended that waggons should not be left without someone in charge. Resolved that if possible the wheels of waggons standing upon the line be secured by chain and lock.'

Sensitive to its rights the Board a few days later had to ponder the novel phenomenon of a police officer trespassing on its property. This was no wild sheep chaser such as Griffith Edwards and the usual Draconian response was not apparent; discretion was the order of the day. The General Manager wrote on June 3rd that Police Sergeant Roberts had 'borrowed a wagon at Aberlefenny and travelled down the line to Corris.' Dix went on to say that he had reported the matter to the Chief Constable but ... 'did not think it advisable to take further action.'

In July 1886 the company was still experiencing trouble with the quarries, principally the Abercwmeiddaw, which had closed anyway, through 'bad trade', and the Abercorris. The latest cheque had bounced and Dix was urgently instructed to retain possession of seven wagonloads of slate, impounded and only to be released on receipt of the rogue cheque.

The Highway Board came to the offensive over the drawing of trucks onto the roadway for delivery purposes. This body had formally banned the practice, despite having accepted 'rent' for it for years, and Dix in an outflanking manoeuvre had convened a vestry meeting (a sort of Parish council) which accordingly 'passed a motion in favour of allowing the trucks on the roads.'

By this time a number of rails on the branches were beginning to wear out and Dix recommended their renewal, buying 150 tons immediately 'at the present low price of £4 per ton.' The Manager at the same time was exhorted to limit expenditure as far as he could 'under all heads, to what is absolutely necessary for the safe passage of the traffic'. Better news came a few weeks later at the end of July with 'indications of improvements in the slate trade.' The Abercwmeiddaw Quarry was to resume operation (if not its payments to the company) and new undertakings would begin at Ratgoed and Cymerau. Further good news came in September, Dix reporting that at a public meeting the Highways Board, cowed, had finally decided in favour of the Corris drawing its trucks onto the roadway. The Corris Board, happy with this victory ordered that the General Manager be informed of 'their satisfaction at his exertions.'

The Chairman, Mr. Lambert, it would seem to have been at this time, and one of the Directors (Mr. Ward) visited the line

Ffridd Wood, at the entrance to the Dulas, provides us with pictures of the line at its most idyllic. H.G.W. Household in The Locomotive, *in August 1926, noted the station here (a grassy mound by 1948) as he passed it in 1925: 'there is a station named Fridd Gate, now closed. The railway follows the Dulas Valley to Abertlefenni and until just short of Corris the route lies alongside the main road'.*

Brian Hilton Collection

on 17th and 18th September 1886. They reported 'the widening of the line between Corris and Aberllefenny was in course of completion and it has been proposed to put down steel rails with the view to extending the passenger traffic to Aberllefenny.' One of the engines 'needed repairs' and a bogie was required for the third engine. This presumably dates the fixing of trailing wheels to the last of the locomotives. Some new cars were wanted and those in use required overhauling ... 'it has been arranged to employ the fitter from the Reading Tramways for the repair of the cars.' His name was Adams and he was compelled to return to Reading in July 1887, having been taken ill.

A heavy storm on the night of 15th October carried off 35 yards of embankment and wall 'near the 3 mile post,' the outcome sending Dix's star plunging back to earth, after its brief ascent upon the victory over the Highways Board. Reconstruction would take about a fortnight during which all traffic would have to stop. Blame hung heavy in the air and it was plainly felt that Dix's original specifications were at fault. A letter was read from George Owen; he had inspected the place and recommended that the foundations of the wall 'should be carried to a lower depth then the General Manager considered necessary and that he must disclaim responsibility for the stability of the work.' Dix was informed of this and rather coldly ordered to confer with Owen, 'and to follow his instructions.' The line reopened for traffic on November 3rd 1886 and the Secretary was despatched to inspect the work, together with Owen.

Abercorris Quarry seems finally to have given up the ghost in November, closing 'for want of funds' and leaving £31.5s.7d owing to the Corris Railway. 'Immediate steps' were instructed for its recovery. The quarry's first reply was to complain of the delay due to the landslip....

The highway problem turned up again, against expectations, for it was considered a vanquished enemy, in January 1887; two of the company's servants 'had been summoned for taking wagons along the road and the summons had been dismissed ... the people in the village were subscribing to defray the Company's expenses.'(!)

By February 1887 the dismal Abercorris was in liquidation and the railway had still not received its money. This did not prevent the official liquidator, Mr. Harvey, demanding the return of the truck seized by Dix. It would be handed over, the Directors replied, a bit loftily, 'immediately on receipt of the amount due.' As a precaution the Board took steps to ascertain where the seizure had taken place. Apparently this had legal implications but comfort was taken from Dix's discovery that the Cambrian had also impounded an Abercorris wagon. Esgairgeiliog station was broken into on 22nd February 1887 and 2 shillings stolen.

By March 1887 the great Extension was proceeding well and Dix reported that the widening of the Abercorris cutting would soon be complete, 'in about a fortnight' (the Corris, or at least Dix, was fond of 'the fortnight' as a measure) with only a retaining wall at Garneddwen 100 yards long by 3 yards and another, 50 yards by 4 yards to be dealt with. 'The Manager proposed to employ 12 additional men so as to get the line completed and ready for passenger traffic by 1st July.' The Board authorised the employment of 5.

Dix had a word with Major Marandin of the Board of Trade who 'promised to facilitate the opening of the line to Aberllefenny' and successfully pressed the chairman upon the number of men needed for completion: 'The chairman has authorised the employment of 12 additional men in order to get the line completed by the end of June.' Matters were complicated in the next weeks, 'several occupiers' of the adjacent land demanding additional level crossings and gates, 'the land having been subdivided since the construction of the line.' The resolution of this once more was to fall upon Dix, 'the Manager to make the best terms.' Further work was needed in any event ... 'it being necessary to provide gatekeeper's lodges at the crossings of roads at Garneddwen and Corris, he has arranged to rent a cottage at the former and has agreed to purchase a small piece of freehold ground at Corris for £5.' The Board cogitated and decided it approved Dix's actions: 'a letter of instructions to the Manager was dictated and ordered to be sent.'

Dix had to write on June 13th that it would not be possible to open the new line until 'sometime in July'; the cost of the unlooked-for gates he had been able to ascertain, 'would be about 15 shillings for the gates and £3 for the crossing, complete'. The Board of Trade he pointed out 'preferred

Slate dressing shed at the Braichgoch, Upper Corris, about 1900. The larger slabs were sawn using the complex of belt drives; once at a manageable size, the traditional 'splitting' into roof slates etc. could begin.

National Library of Wales

Train slipping unobtrusively (this was one of the many qualities of the Corris) through the Dulas landscape, between Maespoeth and Corris. Recorded on a Kodak Brownie, the first houses of Corris lie beyond.

Chris Hawkins Collection

wooden gates to iron', doubtless from a long experience of trains crashing through them.

Dix found a Captain Price to let a cottage at Garneddwen for £5.10s a year 'inclusive of rates and taxes' and he reported the relaying to be 'nearly completed' and the station was also well advanced. 'The operations' he informed the Board 'had been delayed owing to the excessive heat and a scarcity of water.'

The long hot summer wore on; 'July 28th 1887, read Manager's letter of July 27th: The relaying has been completed (to Abellefenny) and also the station ... the fencing will not be finished before the end of the following week. The Corris and Garneddwen level crossings and all the signals and fittings are on the point of completion. The engineers are to commence the survey at once and it is expected that everything will be ready for the Board of Trade inspection by the end of the first week in August.'

Traffic returns lent a further mournful note to this news of delay; 'The passenger traffic continues to show a decrease apparently due to the scarcity of tourists of the district.'

The Aberllefenny Extension was inspected by General Hutchinson on 16th August 1887 and duly approved:

... this extension is a single line 1½ miles long commencing at Corris station and terminating at Aberllefenny, the only new station. No land has been purchased nor any works constructed with a view to the line being doubled. The steepest gradient is 1 in 59 and the sharpest curve has a radius of 5 chains. With the exception of some slight settlement in one of the abutments of the iron bridge which should be carefully watched these works appear to have been substantially built ... there are two public road level crossings protected with proper gates. One of these appears to be authorised but at the other, at five miles four chains, of a side street in Corris, the road should according to the original plan have been diverted and a bridge constructed. This latter crossing has been in existence ever since the line was opened for mineral traffic, now nearly 30 years since, and no objection appears to have been made to it by the local authority, houses having sprung up in its neighbourhood and it would now be a costly and difficult work to carry out the original plan of a road diversion and bridge. By Section 2 of the Act of 1883 the Board of Trade apparently have powers to dispense with this deviation and bridge and under the circumstances I can recommend this power being exercised provided all trains on approaching the level crossing from Aberlefenny are required to stop dead before passing onto the crossing. If the Act is not considered to give this power the company must immediately get the crossing authorised. The points of two siding junctions are locked with the train staff and at Corris and Aberlefenny there are signals interlocked with the points. The requirements are as follows:

1. At Corris. The normal position of the upper points should be for the siding, two of the sidings should be provided with interlocked catch points.

2. At Aberlefenny. A standing signal interlocked with the facing points should be provided, runaway points should be put in above the station.

3. A disc and lamp iron are required for the level crossing gates at 5 miles 54 chains, the line is to be worked with one engine at a time which engine is to carry a staff and an undertaking to this effect is to be provided.

Subject to the remarks about the unauthorised level crossing, to the prompt carrying out of the requirement, of the completion of which the Board of Trade should be informed, and to the receipt of a satisfactory undertaking as to the mode of working, the opening of the extension of the Corris Railway from Corris to Aberllefenny is recommended.

This was whirlwind stuff, given past encounters between the BoT and the Corris; the new line was open for passenger traffic 'on the morning of 25th,' whilst Dix could write on the 13th September ... 'the requirements .. are well in hand.' The Directors wrote to express their satisfaction with the way in which he worked.

The old protagonist, 'the road', took issue with the Corris again in the autumn of 1887 and Dix had to report that the company had been summoned by the Road Surveyor, for not providing a lodge at the crossing 300 yards below Llwyngwern station: the keys of the gates were kept at a cottage close by but the surveyor wished them kept at another cottage, for £2.12s per annum. 'The Manager had employed Mr. Rowland and the case had been decided in favour of the company but without costs.'

'The whole of the Board of Trade requirements' would be completed during the week, Dix reported in October; he had dispensed with the extra men excepting two or three who would be paid off in about a fortnight. Just after this, at the beginning of November, the undertaking was given to the Board of Trade regarding the system of working to be employed between Corris and Aberllefenny, 'only one engine in steam or two engines coupled .. employed at any one time and that such engines shall at all times carry the train staff for that section.' These were weighty matters and on the latter the Common Seal of the company 'was affixed thereto.'

Gross earnings for the Extension for a three month period were totted up on 15th December 1887 and found to be '£57.16.5d, 3,719 passengers having been carried, an average of 286 passengers at £4.8s.11d per week.'

Trucks concerned the Directors once more in December and the hostage Abercorris example, it was decided, could safely be put to use if Dix took care 'to retain possession of it.' The company was however £3.10s out of pocket when an Abercorris wagon went out of control and crashed. It 'had got loose while being coupled and overturned, smashing the slates'. Dix paid for the damage.

On 31st April 1888 comes the first mention of a break for Dix, a separate item in the Directors Minutes, entitled 'Managers Holiday.' He asked for a leave of absence from April 28th to May 14th which was 'granted' without obvious demur. The Minutes do not record if he was paid, but presumably he did not spend it on the Corris Grand Tour. This was to form Dix's customary hols.

Dix came back, no doubt refreshed, but to find one of the horses had gone lame. He proposed to sell it and required two for the *Talyllyn Wagonette*, a two horse passenger vehicle. Mr. Morrison of the Sunderland Tramways was to 'be employed to purchase two.' Dix on his return was also able to calculate the Extension income: 'for 40 weeks from August 25th 1887 to May 31st 1888 ... had been £158.4s.10½d, from 10,176 passengers, an average of £3.19s.11.2d per week'.

Water was long a problem at Machynlleth and despite frequent floods the engine supply was inadequate. Dix as ever saw to this and had a 'tube well' put down. He had thereby 'obtained a good supply of water for the engines'. A tank was of course necessary, 'the cost of a slate one being £5.15s or a galvanised iron one £4.11s, the latter being more suitable'. It is not necessary to indicate which choice the directors made. The directors were also suddenly aware of the high interest charged for the Corris account and wrote a sharp letter to the bank in July 1888; in response the rate was halved (these were far off times indeed) to ⅛%. The following month however Dix asked for an increase in salary. The chairman and Col. Gourley would 'visit Corris the following week'. They were presumably happy with what they saw and ordered an increase in August, to £200 per annum.

Though each was dependent upon the other there is in the Corris Minutes almost no reference to indicate any degree of affability, or even accord, between the railway and the quarries. Communications never rise much above the level of some sort of 'demand', usually for money. On 6th September

1888 the Directors heard of further malice, this time on the part of the Cymerau Quarry: 'the debris from this quarry was being tipped alongside the river opposite to the line and several large blocks had rolled into the stream diverting it and causing it to undermine the line. The Manager of the quarry had declined to interfere but the underground Manager had since undertaken to take steps to remedy the danger threatened.' By November the debris had been cleared 'sufficiently to avert danger to the line.'

The 1880s was the formative decade of the Corris; during those years the great Extension was completed and the company established itself as a 'railway proper', with Dix attending London conferences of 'lesser line' managers. The railway (you couldn't really get much of a 'lesser line' than the Corris) was perhaps at its most active then; dynamic would never be a word to associate with the Corris and its doings but it did seem to have a pioneering, frontier spirit in those times. The stuff of everyday life remained of course the constant parochialism of squabbles and the threat of court action. One senses that Dix enjoyed these years best though in the 1890s and into the new century (ominously for Dix) it seems the Board, and particularly the Managing Director, took a firmer hold of matters.

The 1880s ended typically with a flurry of actions, orders and minor cockups. On 29th November 1889 the Board heard the curious case of the Revd. O.J. Williams, 'curate in charge of Corris'. The local lark was obviously to charge about in trucks and the unfortunate Williams was described (startling indeed in a man of the cloth) as having 'jumped on a wagon behind

On the left, the great man, J.R. Dix, in his retirement years, long after leaving the Dulas.

Chris Hawkins Collection

Corris Express, Machynlleth.

'The Corris Express' at Machynlleth. The Corris station lay alongside but below the Cambrian (later Great Western) station and for such a tiny concern had a remarkable straggling organisation. The General Manager's Office was removed to Machynlleth from Corris, whilst the Secretary resided in Bristol, 'a rather divided executive' as Household remarks.

Brian Hilton Collection

the 12.15 down train on 30th October when passing Maespoeth Junction.' Class played an important part in these matters, or else fear of the Almighty, and Dix was reluctant for this early example of clerical railway interest to go further: 'consideration of the matter' should be postponed he felt, 'pending further report.' Nothing more is recorded of the matter, not even a quiet word to the Bishop. At the same Board meeting a much clearer case came to light, fortunately it concerned 3rd class passengers and there was never any doubt as to how to proceed against that type of person. Two wretches had been found riding 1st class with 3rd class tickets. They were whisked off to court but the magistrate had confounded the railway by *dismissing* the case, though the pair were ordered to pay costs of some £7-£8, a matter, probably, of several weeks wages in the Dulas valley.

An incident wholly more serious (to the corporate mind of the Corris Railway at least) and an even more startling contrast to the affairs of the policeman and the curate came in November. Dix writing to his Board on 27th noted solemnly that 'three persons connected with the Dulas Slate Co. had stopped a train by holding up a red pocket handkerchief for the purpose of travelling by it.' The train that is, not the handkerchief; now they had probably done this every week for years but the Corris took an extremely dim view. 'It being an offence *punishable by two years imprisonment* [author's italics] they had offered to pay four guineas to the railway Benevolent trust and a further guinea for legal expenses, which the Manager had agreed to accept.' Dix later proposed giving only half to the Benevolent Institution and half 'for the benefit of the poor'. The Victorians seemed often to be like that. They lived in harsher times altogether but looking after one's own was often by some means achieved. If transgression meant swift retribution than fealty should be rewarded. The Corris more than once continued to pay the full wages of staff injured in their duties and a humble gatekeeper in his 'seventies 'now too infirm' received a small pension.

More troubles followed the incident of the red handkerchief – two men in charge of a trolley at Maespoeth Bank 'had allowed it to run down the line smashing the gates at Evan's Bridge and damaging those at Llwyngwern finally stopping in Ffridd Wood without causing further damage. The men have been dismissed'. Within weeks the station master at Esgairgeiliog was in trouble; Dix had discovered 'irregularities in Evans' accounts, he having collected two amounts without accounting for them. The Manager had severely reprimanded Evans and the money had been paid. Resolved: that the Manager be informed that the Board take a serious view of such delinquency and had the circumstances been reported earlier would have directed the dismissal of Evans.' In January 1889 Dix was 'instructed to exercise a closer supervision over the station master's accounts.' Dix had quite clearly saved the man's bacon.

Locomotive coal prices went up that month by 3 shillings a ton, though Dix had with careful husbandry laid in 20 tons and had a further two wagon loads on the way at the old price. It was all contributing to the slow decline of the Corris accounts and further bad news came with word that the Dulas Slate Co. was in difficulties. They still owed for some old rails and slate carriage and Dix needless to say 'was taking steps to obtain payment.' The slate company inevitably defaulted and Dix resorted to the usual device, seizing and impounding two loads of slate.

Something called the Railway and Canal Traffic Act loomed large in the next few months. It required companies to prepare classifications of traffic and schedules of rates and for a time brought the Corris into the dizzy orbit of the larger companies and the *Railway Association,* no less. Prescribed notices had to be inserted in *The London Gazette* and the rather more obscure *Oswestry Advertiser* but the Board were glum at the statutory £50 demanded by the Board of Trade 'for expenses.' Naturally the local traders were ill-disposed to the revised rates and this embroiled Dix in all sorts of further exertions and soothing noises. The Board of Trade at least proved sympathetic and indicated a willingness to settle for £25 but a circular later in the year warned that the company would have to comply with the Regulation of Railways Act 1888. This meant having the fare printed or written on every passenger ticket from 1st July 1890 and an obligation to adopt the continuous brake. Dix complied with the first condition easy enough but reassured the Directors with thoughts that the Board of Trade would not insist on the brakes. The renowned Henry Oakley of the Great Northern was in communication with Dix, who actually went to meet him in London regarding representation to the Board of Trade. The Corris Directors were shy of this; it meant joining the Railway Association but they became enthusiastic enough at Oakley's suggestions that the Corris 'entrance fee' be in proportion to their gross receipts relative to other companies, and therefore miniscule. Dix doubtless bought a new coat for the occasion.

Trains were 'greatly delayed' in February through snowstorms but in a meeting with the Dulas Slate Co. creditors Dix reckoned to have sufficient goods impounded to cover the bill, £16.13s.9d. Further encouragement was that Mr. William Roberts had admitted liability for £10 due on some old rails.

In May the company even made a subscription to the Corris brass band and in July was forced to approve about £17.10s for new water pipes at the Maespoeth engine shed, the old ones having badly corroded.

Dix 'on the ground' at Corris could get matters sorted with a minimum of fuss and usually to the satisfaction of all, except when retribution was involved. He was apparently well-liked in the Valley and round about and had a sympathy for the locals, very few of whom spoke English at all in the 1880s and 1890s. Dix taught himself Welsh, for an Englishman in such a position a quite exceptional step. At the same time as arranging for Lewis, the 77-year old gatekeeper to receive a pension, he drew the Board's attention (August 1889) to the need for a gatekeeper's dwelling at Evans Bridge. This could be put up for £100 and be occupied by a platelayer whose wife would attend the gates. In August one of the horses 'working the Talyllyn car' had been laid off with a sore shoulder but Dix 'assured the Board it was recovering'.

On 18th September another child was killed on the railway, Laura Pugh Davies. She had strayed onto the Braichgoch branch to be run down by two wagons rounding a curve. A verdict of accidental death was recorded, the jury recommending 'that the men in charge of wagons be enjoined to use great caution in descending the inclines.' The Board of Trade wrote to the company about fencing the line and this Dix duly arranged.

A new firm, Ashton Green Matthews & Co. set up in the valley in the autumn of 1889, something of an event and a new siding was to be put in at their expense, £91 for one 'in lieu of the old machine siding.'

Profits in 1889 were at least good for the Talyllyn car: 'the receipts from the Talyllyn and Posting Traffic had amounted this year to £110.10s.6d against £57.15s.3d during 1888 and the Manager recommended the purchase of an additional wagonette to carry 10 passengers, which he could purchase for £35.15s. Resolved that the particulars of the costs of working the traffic be obtained.'

The 1880s had seen the Corris develop into a steam railway; a solid if not exactly flourishing Victorian business and the decade ended with hope for the unpredictable slate trade. Even the errant Abercorris was 'reconstructed' under a Mr. Ochard and Mr. Edward Lee, of Basinghall Street. They had asked for a monthly carriage account but the Corris was wary, and one of the Directors, Mr. Fraser, was requested to make enquiry 'as to Mr. Lee's position.' The quarry restarted work in December 1889 (the Director pursued enquiries 'as to its stability with the National Provincial Bank') and the Braichgoch went over to full time working. Things were looking up.

The new decade began as typical Corris drama, with the usual ingredients – local conflict, a clash of class, a dashing intercession from Dix and the sombre consideration of the Board. The episode encapsulates much of what the Corris was about ...

Read Manager's letter of February 5th; Richard Davis, Station Master at Lluyngwern had been charged by Col. Norris's keeper with poaching while looking after some wood which he had brought from Mr. Gillart's woodman. He had been summoned and fined 6s and costs. The Manager had information that both the charge and the magistrate's decision were unjust; Col. Norris wished that the man should be discharged, the Manager however stated that Davies had been a good servant to the Company and had been unjustly charged. Resolved: that Davies be retained in the service.

Soon afterwards the Board of Trade was in the Dulas again, Dix writing on February 5th 1900 with the information that 'the siding called the Machine Siding on the Corris Railway has been removed slightly lower down the line and a trap point has been put in one chain from the points. It is still secured by an Annetts patent lock.' Colonel Rich duly inspected ... 'a new siding junction and carriage points are locked by a key which forms a part of the train staff with which the railway is worked. The junction is on a steep gradient and the Company undertake only to stop at the siding to put in or take out wagons when the engine is at the lower or south end of the train. The connection rods should be fixed by lock or a set of split pins instead of with a split pin only and the stock rails should be secured to gauge with a tie bar. Subject to this being done I can recommend the sanction of the Board of Trade ...'

There was some concern in February 1890, for the Board of Trade had written under the Regulation of Railways Act 1889, with a draft order 'as to the adoption of the block system interlocking at points, signals and continuous brakes'. This was immediately referred to Dix and a request for exemption from the continuous brakes order was applied for ... 'due to the peculiar circumstances [heavily underlined in the Minutes] of the line.'

The Corris was gripped almost from its beginnings by the rising costs and declining revenues which were to stifle it at the last. In April 1890 the platelayers applied for a wage increase of 1s a week and 'in addition desired to be allowed to cease work at 1 o'clock on Saturdays.' Mr. Dix offered to ascertain the hours and rates paid by the Cambrian Railways 'and to place the Corris men on the same footing.' He was presumably aware that the Cambrian conditions were at least not worse than those prevailing upon the Corris. Troubles continued with the Abercorris Quarry; this account had drifted overdue to £47.8s.8d, a vast sum if related to platelayers wages. £23 was all the quarry could come up with. It was nearly June before the company coughed up and then only settled its account up to the end of March!

An interesting side effect of the Railway Canal Traffic Act turned up in June 1890; the Corris had been issuing 'Traders tickets' to the quarry managers and under the Act such preference was prohibited. Anyone, it transpired, was entitled to such a ticket on demand, should such a facility exist, and the practice was discontinued with some haste. This presumably did little to further relations with the quarries. The Aberllefenny bridge was ordered to be repaired in wood, the old timbers having rotted, in October 1890. The Directors suggested iron girders but shrank from the costs provided by Dix.

Dix had bad news towards the end of September; a tube burst (the engine is not specified) ... 'while running the 6.40am up train on 25th September, delaying the train 2 hours. It would be advisable to have the third engine put into thorough repair. It was, Resolved, that an estimate of the cost be obtained.' The engine duly went off to Loughborough, via the Cambrian on a flat wagon.

At the end of 1890 the Board of Trade once again cast its shadow; it was nice for Dix to rub shoulders with those in the higher reaches of the railway world, a heady experience no doubt but increasing regulation brought with it a financial cost. In November the Corris Board met to hear the latest missive from the BoT ... 'with the order made ... upon the Company in pursuance of their Act, to adopt the Block system within 12 months, to provide for the Interlocking of points and signals within 18 months, and to provide Continuous Brakes for all trains within 3 years from the 20th November.' At the same meeting letters of November 25th, 28th and December 3rd were read from Dix, reporting that 'he had had an interview with Mr. Courtenay Boyle and had obtained an extension of the time for providing brakes from 2 to 3 years. Mr. Boyle had also promised that the Company should be exempted from the obligation to adopt the Block system in consideration of their only working one engine in steam, or two or more coupled together. Mr. Dix recommended that the engine about to be repaired should be fitted with the automatic brake and that the six old carriages be fitted upon three

Quarry workers and dogs, posing on a slab wagon, Ratgoed

new bogie frames, at the rate of one new frame per year, to be fitted with the brake apparatus; the cost of fitting the brake being £50 per engine, £15 per carriage and £20 for the guard's van. He recommended that the vacuum automatic Brake be adopted. Resolved, that the Manager's recommendations be adopted subject to the brake being in accordance with the Board of Trade requirements.'

The early part of the following year, 1890, was spent in more accustomed fashion, as the usual disputatious exchanges rustled through the Dulas. These characteristically rumbled on; the Braichgoch Co. for instance began a sally modestly enough, though Dix was too alert for them. Would the Corris, the Secretary of the Braichgoch enquired, 'be prepared to purchase their wagons and provide same in future; and also whether they would be willing to enter into an agreement to relinquish the agreement for haulage at any future time and restore the Braichgoch Co. to their present position? The Braichgoch had stubbornly been working its own trains on the line; it being cheaper, it naturally desired to continue the practice. Dix recommended 'that such an agreement be not entered into', contending 'that they have no Parliamentary right to perform their own haulage.' It was 'Resolved' that, 'the Manager be desired to point out by what Act the original right of uses of the line by the Braichgoch Co. has been abrogated.'

Further legal ponderings followed: 'the Act of 1858 did not confer upon the Braichgoch Co. the right to use the line but that it incorporated the Railways Clauses Consolidation Act 1845 under Sec 92 of which, upon payment of the tolls from time to time demandable all companies and persons shall be entitled to use the Railway with *engines and* carriages properly constructed. Mr. Godreys letter of 13th January 1887 was also read in which he stated his opinion that under Clause 9 of the Corris Railway Act 1880 the Company have the right to

Corris servant at Machynlleth new station around 1910.

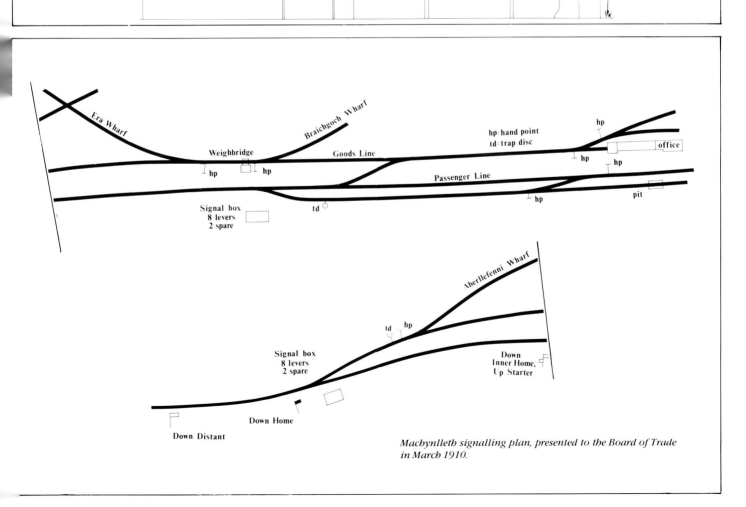

Dix's arrangements 'for the proposed station at Esgairgeiliog and Llwyngwern' signed by him and dated 28th November 1883. Details seemed to vary as the buildings were actually put up, or modifications were made in succeeding years.

fireplace

seat

open front

1 ft

Era Wharf

Braichgoch Wharf

Weighbridge

Goods Line

hp = hand point
td = trap disc

office

hp

hp

hp

hp

hp

Passenger Line

hp

pit

Signal box
8 levers
2 spare

td

Aberllefenni Wharf

td   hp

Signal box
8 levers
2 spare

Down
Inner Home,
Up Starter

Down Home

Down Distant

Machynlleth signalling plan, presented to the Board of Trade in March 1910.

No.3 at Aberllefenni in August 1930. By the time of Household's visit in 1925 the daily train service consisted of three down and three up trains between Aberllefenni and Machynlleth, with an evening train from Aberllefenni to Corris. 'On Monday mornings there is an extra train down and up, and on Monday, Wednesday and Saturday evenings a train each way between Machynlleth and Corris. Journey times vary from half an hour to forty minutes for the 6½ miles, not very fast running, but there is usually a stop of several minutes at Corris and then again at Maespoeth engine shed, as well as the halts at the two remaining intermediate stations.

R.G. Jarvis

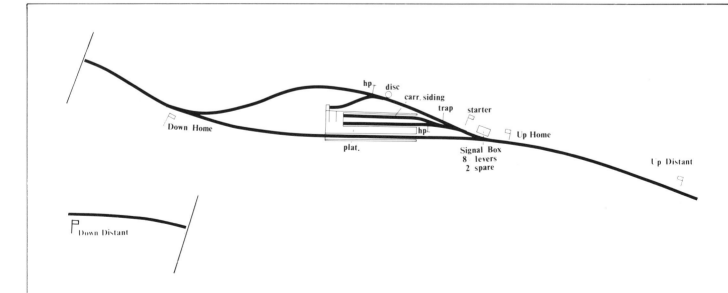

Signalling diagram of Corris, dated March 1910.

The archetypal Corris train.

prevent the Braichgoch Co. from carrying their slates over any portion of the line open for passenger traffic: It was Resolved that notice be given to the Braichgoch Co. that from and after the 30th June next they will not be permitted to convey traffic over any part of the main line and that this Co. will be prepared to convey such traffic at the statutory rates: Ordered, that a letter to the Braichgoch Co. be prepared and submitted to the next Board Meeting.

The slate Co. remained unmoved by this and in April it was resolved that a Notice be issued, 'to discontinue their haulage by horses on the main line from 30th June.' With this the Braichgoch began to cave in; the Corris Secretary met with its Directors on June 5th and it was 'mutually agreed that the haulage should be performed by the Corris from 1st July at 2s per ton.' Triumph.

William Williams experienced Corris justice in December 1890; summoned for some un-named offence he had agreed, in return for the summons being withdrawn, to pay 20s 'and to allow bills stating his offences to be printed.'

The line was flooded 'to a great depth' on November 24th 'preventing the running of the incoming trains beyond Ffrydd Gate.'

The poor old Abercorris expired again in the early summer of 1891. The Aberllefenny quarries suffered a brief strike in October and in January 1892 all the quarries made complaints of delay, the line being blocked by snowstorms.

The slate trade generally bore out the optimism expressed at the end of the 1880s and Dix wrote to the Board in January 1892, 'stating that the slate traffic continued very satisfactorily principally from the Braichgoch and Aberllefenny quarries.' It is actually rather difficult to divine the true state of affairs for Dix writes in August bemoaning the level of business. It 'continued in a depressed state but the passenger traffic was improving.'

The Board got into a bit of a spat, with Dix at loggerheads with the Cambrian, in 1892. On June 2nd news had come of arrangements made by the Cambrian for 'a coach to run from Towyn to Talyllyn Lake from 1st June and (Mr Dix) has heard that they were trying to arrange for a coach to be run from Machynlleth, through Corris. to the Lake.' Dix declared that the Corris' own Talyllyn service should be commenced, in the circumstances, from 1st June and this arrangement had already been concluded, with the chairman's approval. Dix in addition passed on correspondence between himself and Mr. Vaughan, passenger superintendent of the Cambrian Railways; he (Vaughan) considered 'that there had been an understanding that the conveyances from Corris to Talyllyn should not be commenced until July 1st and he now declined to issue cheap through tickets from the Coast to Corris as formerly by more than one train a day.' This was potentially serious and the Board determined 'that the Manager be desired to see Mr. Vaughan and endeavour to restore the relations of the two companies to a friendly footing...'

Nothing could be calculated to stir the Board more than the prospect of such an upset but Dix failed to move with sufficient alacrity: 'June 16th 1892 ... The Secretary was instructed to intimate to the Manager that the Board are dissatisfied at having no further report from him as to this matter, and to desire that a General Report be furnished for the information of every Board meeting. Dix was soon back: 'the misunderstanding' with Mr. Vaughan of the Cambrian 'had been satisfactorily arranged...' the big neighbour had agreed to issue through tickets to Corris 'and had also arranged for a circular tour from their Coast stations via Corris and Towyn.' Receipts, moreover, from the Talyllyn traffic, 'had been £16.19s.9d up to 25th June; the Manager desired authority to purchase two more horses if the traffic should require it and it was resolved that 2 horses be purchased if necessary'

THE FINEST COACH TOUR IN WALES.

Cader Idris and Tal-y-llyn Lake.

Time Table for JULY, AUGUST & SEPTEMBER, 1907.

			a.m.	a.m.	p.m.	p.m.	p.m.	p.m.
Aberllefenny	..dep.	..	7m 5	10 0	12 20	1 55	4 45	..
Garneddwen	,,	..	a	a	a	a	a	..
Corris	..arr.	..	7m13	10 8	12 28	2 3	4 53	..

					a m.			
TALYLLYN LAKE by Coach ..	..dep.	..	..	..	11 20	1 0	3 50	5 0
Corris ,, ..	..arr.	..	..	..	12 20	2 0	4 50	6 10

		a.m.	a.m.	a m.	p.m.	p.m.	p.m.	p.m.
Corris	..dep.	5m35	7 15	10 10	12 30	2 5	5 0	6 20
Esgairgeiliog	.. ,,	a	7 22	a	12 37	2 12	5 7	6 27
Llwyngwern	.. ,,	a	7 29	a	12 44	2 19	5 14	6 34
Ffridd Gate (for Llanwrin)..	.. ,,	a	a	a	a	a	a	a
Machynlleth	..arr.	6 15	7 40	10 35	12 55	2 30	5 25	6 45

		a.m.	a.m.	a.m.	p.m.	p.m.	p.m.	p.m.
Machynlleth	..dep.	6 25	9 5	11 15	1 15	2 55	5 40	7 20
Ffridd Gate (for Llanwrin) ..	.. ,,	a	a	a	a	a	a	a
Llwyngwern	.. ,,	6 37	9 17	11 27	1 27	3 7	5 52	7 32
Esgairgeiliog	.. ,,	6 43	9 23	11 33	1 33	3 13	5 58	7 38
Corris (for Cader Idris and Talyllyn Lake)	arr.	6 50	9 30	11 40	1 40	3 20	6 5	7 45

			a.m.	a.m.	p.m.	p.m.		
Corris by Coach	...dep.	..	9 35	11 45	1 45	3 25	..	..
TALYLLYN LAKE ..	..arr.	..	10 20	12 30	2 30	4 10	..	..

		a.m.	a.m.	a.m.	p.m.	p.m.		p.m.
Corris	..dep.	6m52	9 32	11 42	1 42	3 22	..	7 47
Garneddwen	.. ,,	a	a	a	a	a	..	a
Aberllefenny	..arr.	7m 0	9 40	11 50	1 50	3 30	..	7 55

a *Stops if required, passengers to inform guard.* **m** *Mondays only.*

Delightful Day or Half-Day Rail and Coach Outing.—From June 1st Conveyances will run at times as above between CORRIS and TALYLLYN LAKE, landing Passengers close to the foot of the Minfford Ascent, and allowing ample time for ascending CADER IDRIS. Fares—(By Coach), Single Journey, 1s.

Cheap Day Return Tickets are issued to Talyllyn Lake, Corris and Aberllefenny, from Aberystwyth, Borth, Aberdovey, Towyn, Barmouth, Dolgelley, Criccieth, Pwllheli, etc.

Cheap Day Return Tickets are issued to Talyllyn Lake from Whitchurch, Ellesmere, Oswestry, Llanymynech, Welshpool, Montgomery, Newtown, Llanidloes, Moat Lane, &c.

The Company give notice that they do not undertake that the Talyllyn Coaches shall start or arrive at the times specified in the Time Table, nor will they be responsible for any loss or inconvenience which may arise from delay, detention or injury of any nature. A limited number of Passengers only can be conveyed by each Coach and those having Through Rail and Coach Tickets will get precedence; those holding such 1st Class Tickets getting also preference to the Box Seats.

A Corris wagonette (top) by Talyllyn Lake in the early 1900s. Third class passengers and, if they proved not up to the task, their second class companions, according to the rules, could be asked to push in case of difficulty. Those enjoying 1st class could decline such indignity. In 1892 the Corris had inaugurated 'circular tours' with the Cambrian, 'from their coast stations via Corris and Towyn' and throughout the 1890s the wagonette traffic was encouraging: 'additional stabling,' Dix declared, would be necessary at Corris. The charabanc (below) is a fascinating contrast, the occupants' demeanour reminiscent today of Suzuki jeep passengers.

Brian Hilton Collection

GREAT WESTERN RAILWAY

COMBINED RAIL & ROAD TOURS

From Barmouth

EVERY WEEK DAY, EXCEPT WHERE OTHERWISE SHOWN

JULY 7th to SEPTEMBER 20th, 1930.

TO	Tour No.	Outward Trains.	Return Fares 3rd Class	Returning same day.
		a.m. p.m. p.m.	s. d.	
Talyllyn Lake (via Machynlleth and Corris)	1	9 45 12 23 2 20	6 0	2.15, 3.55, or 5.20 p.m. from Talyllyn Lake.
Dolgelley, Talyllyn Lake and Corris	2a	10S20 12 30 2 40	4 9	1.23, 4.26, or 5.38 p.m. from Machynlleth.
Corris, Talyllyn Lake and Towyn, to Corris by Rail, thence by Road to Towyn, home by Rail	21	9.45 12.23 2.20	6 0	Any Train from Towyn
Towyn, Talyllyn Lake, and Corris, to Towyn by Rail, thence Road to Corris, home by Rail.	21a	9.45 12.23 2 20	6 0	Any Train from Machynlleth
Dolgelley and Dinas Mawddwy	20a	10S20 a.m., 1 18 p.m.	4 6	12.40 or 3.10 p.m. from Dinas Mawddwy.
Beddgelert (via Portmadoc and Road Motor)	3	9 35 a.m.	4 6	3.0 p.m. from Beddgelert.
Around Snowdon to Llanberis, via Portmadoc and Road Motor, returning via Caernarvon to Portmadoc	4	9 35 a.m.	7 0	3.0 p.m. from Llanberis.
Llanberis, for Ascent of Snowdon, via Portmadoc and Road Motor	4a	9 35 a.m., 12 22 p.m.	7 0	4.15 or 6.30 p.m. from Llanberis
Snowdon Summit, by Mountain Railway, via Portmadoc and Road Motor	5	12 22 p.m.	13 0	6.30 p.m. from Llanberis.
Bettws-y-Coed and Fairy Glen, via Portmadoc & Road Motor (Tuesdays, Thursdays and Saturdays)	6	9 35 a.m.	7 0	3.0 p.m. from Bettws-y-Coed.
The Isle of Anglesey Circular Tour, via Portmadoc and Road Motor (Mondays, Wednesdays and Fridays only)	30	9.35 a.m.	10 0	2.30 p.m. from Holyhead.
Nevin	7	9 35 a.m., 12 22 p.m.	5 6	3.3, 4.30, 5.30 6.0 p.m.
Abersoch	8	9 35 a.m., 12 22 p.m.	5 9	3.0, 3.30, 4.30, 5.30 p.m.
Aberdaron	9	9 35 a.m., 12 22 p.m.	7 3	3.0 or 5.0 p.m.
Bethesda Loop Tour, via Portmadoc and Road Motor (Mondays, Wednesdays and Fridays only)	10	9 35 a.m.	8 0	6.0, 7.15 or 8.25 p.m. from Portmadoc.

For full particulars and Map of District, see Tours Programme.   S—On Saturdays leave Barmouth at 10.32 a.m.

Rail and Walking Tours.—For particulars see Tours Programme obtainable at all Stations.

HOLIDAY SEASON TICKETS—REDUCED RATES.

Available for any number of journeys and for break of journey at any intermediate station.

	Available between						Fare, 3rd Class
No. 5	Aberystwyth, Barmouth and Dolgelley						10/-
No. 6	Pwllheli, Barmouth and Dolgelley						10/-
No. 7	Pwllheli, Dolgelley and Aberystwyth						15/-
No. 8	Pwllheli, Blaenau Festiniog and Barmouth						10/-

Two Corris motorbuses 'at a fair lick' over the Talyllyn Pass and below, a Great Western charabanc at the Braichgoch Inn, in July 1928. The line of roadside rails, easily missed at a glance, indicates the horse worked portion from Upper Corris to Maespoeth Junction.

Brian Hilton Collection, National Library of Wales

Chapter Five
Failing Fortunes

A flurry of Board changes occurred in 1892. In August, with not all the directors present (though a full house, it must be said, was seldom attained), Mr. James Clifton Robinson was appointed Managing Director 'with power to make such traffic and other arrangements as may be necessary'. At the same meeting the next item concerned the resignation of one of the directors, Mr. Ward. This was accepted 'on the motion of Mr. Godfray seconded by Mr. Robinson,' (who had not appeared on the Board so far). It was resolved 'that Mr. Geo. White be and is hereby elected Chairman of the company.' A coup?

Col. Gourley, who presumably voted with Ward in the minority 3:2, resigned in September. The Secretary followed in November and it was resolved that the offices be moved to Clare Street House, Bristol.

The new Managing Director brought a change in working to the Corris and from the Minutes it is clear that Robinson, compared to his predecessor, involved himself much more in the day to day affairs of the company. Dix had always bought and sold the various horses for instance; this was usually accomplished at a loss, though such an outcome was only to be expected of course. Horses in Dix's time served much like motor vehicles now; the Corris dealt second hand (probably it was more like third, fourth or fifth hand) in the beasts, precisely in the manner of motors today and each transaction, and the work extracted, lowered the 'selling on' price. The ultimate ending place was of course that original scrap yard, the knackers. Now, Robinson, far removed from the Dulas, claimed such wholly local tasks. Dix, sensing perhaps the shadows lengthening on his career, still *did* everything but whatever routine sales, purchases and orders he might make in a month in the Dulas was now declared as the 'Managing Directors Report.'

The Corris, late in its life, passed to the Great Western, but the Directors early on determined upon getting rid of it; it was to be leased to the Cambrian and the blessing of the Board was first apparent from 30th October 1893. It was 'unanimously approved', talks having gone on for 'some months past.' There was a hiccup, for on 19th August 1894 Messrs. Fraser, the solicitors, wrote that 'the negotiation had not advanced, the matter now awaiting the consideration and attention of the Cambrian Chairman.' By 13th June 1895 it was apparent that more than a hiccup was involved, and the Chairman read details of what had now become 'the *suggested* leasing' of the line; reporting that the Cambrian Directors 'did not see their way to accept the Company's suggested terms he, (the Chairman) had put an end to the negociations' [sic]. By the end of 1896 the Chairman reported upon 'correspondence' (undisclosed) with the Great Western 'on the sale of the railway.'

Dix (he had once worked on the Cambrian and would be in touch daily, on a local basis) had obviously got wind of the Director's efforts to off-load the Corris. It is hard not to imagine a slow decline in relations between the General Manager and his Board and Dix's cause was not helped when he offered to lease the line himself. It was not a gesture the Board appreciated ... 'On a report that Mr Dix, the Manager, had applied to the Managing Director inquiring as to the possibility of the Line being leased to him personally, the Secretary was instructed to write to Mr. Dix expressing the view of the Board that assuming from his application he was under the impression he could work the Railway to better

advantage, they expected him to exercise all his energies for the Company's benefit.' A chill wind blew in the Dulas for Dix that night.

The Dovey Bridge, the line's principal engineering feature, was found to be 'in an unsatisfactory state of repair' in August 1894 and 'on the recommendation of the Engineer, Mr. George Owen, the necessary repairs had been authorised at a estimated cost of £8.5s for materials, the Company's men doing the work.

The Directors, or rather two of them, met in London in November 1895 and January 1896, Mr. White and Mr. Godfray. They were put out at losing a court action brought by Williams & Co. for damages and costs arising from the death of a mare, killed by a train after it had jumped the very fence designed to keep it out. It is hard not to have sympathy with White and Godfray: 'It seemed a very extraordinary decision but the Managing Director understood there was no chance of appealing successfully.'

In 1900 Dix, in what had become a formality, requested his usual fortnight holiday, in his favourite period, 21st April to 5th May. It was turned down by the MD ...

In 1902 the Managing Director *demanded* a report from Dix in explanation of the 'considerable shrinkage' in traffic receipts. An 'explanation of the causes of the falling off' was required and Dix's report, now unfortunately long lost to us was 'laid before the Board' on 31st January. Profit for that year at least did not show a dramatic decline; at nearly £800 it was indeed an advance on many previous years. The dividend dropped to 5%; it had been 6% for a few years with highs of 8% or 9% in the 1870s but it had been much lower, 3% or 4% or less. The following year profits rose again to over £900 and the 6% dividend was restored.

Dix asked for an increase in salary, the first for years, in August 1902 but 'it was decided not to grant the application.'

The estrangement of Dix and the Board seemed to have a reflection, or an echo, in broader relations between Corris and Bristol. In November 1902 an unprecedented *Petition* arrived 'signed by a number of the inhabitants of Corris with regard to cheap fares and the running of an early morning train to Machynlleth. It was decided to obtain the observations of the Manager on the subject before replying.' What Dix said is not recorded and in the subsequent deliberations of the Board there is no further reference to his comments. The Petition came up for further consideration in February 1903, when the Board declared 'the existing fares could not be altered and that inasmuch as the winter service of trains was now in operation the grounds of complaint as to the time of running the incoming trains were removed.' So there.

Abercwmeiddaw ('probably the most successful quarry on the entire length of the Broad Vein'– *Return to Corris*, Avon Anglia 1988, anon) was also unhappy with the Corris services at this time. The Manager corresponded at length with the Corris Secretary, anxious for a 'deduction of a portion of the account on the grounds of excessive charges.' The Corris was insistent though, and in December 1903 replied: 'the Company were not prepared to allow the deductions, as the charges made were authorised by Act of Parliament and that unless they adopted a more reasonable attitude, prepayment of any freight for conveyance must be insisted on.' This was not exactly the essence of cordiality and there was further bad tidings. Dix had written, presumably in an attempt to placate

Robinson and his Board before the event, warning them to expect a drop in traffic from the Braichgoch Quarry. He described 'a large fall of rock' presumably obscuring the working face, and intimating that 'reduced freights for conveyance on the Company's line would result therefrom.'

Profits nevertheless remained well over £900 in 1903, allowing the usual 6% dividend but by December 1904 with the annual accounts looming one of the Directors, Samuel White, was in touch with Dix, expressing anxiety at a drop in business. He bent Dix's ear somewhat and extracted a promise from him 'to use his utmost efforts to try to substantially reduce the decrease before the end of the year.' Profits that year were £641.8s.7d with the dividend 4%.

Payment difficulties seem to have worsened as the new century wore on and were routinely reported in an almost weary fashion. Instead of the usual detailed pursuit of particular miscreants the Secretary simply referred to 'the various slate quarries [it is difficult not to believe they acted in covert concert] with regard to outstanding accounts for carriage of slates' ... 'Steps were being taken to obtain payment' but a month later in November 1905 several of the accounts remained outstanding, though the Secretary 'was doing everything possible to obtain payment.' Profit for 1905 crashed to £202.16s.9d, with a dividend rate of 1%.

The Managing Director, Robinson, reported at a gloomy meeting in Bristol on 19th October 1906. The recent disappointing returns were due largely to very adverse trade conditions in connection with the slate quarries, but 'he was doing everything he could to keep down the working expenses and secure wherever possible new traffic.' In this dismal atmosphere a proposal from the Ratgoed Quarry, for a reduction in charges, could hardly enjoy much prospect of success. 'The existing rate from that quarry being reasonable, the application for a reduction was refused.'

There now comes one of the most extraordinary episodes to be revealed in the Corris Minutes, the sad business, after many successful and worthwhile years, of Dix's departure. It began with a rather unpleasant communication from William

Inside the Braichgoch dressing shed.

Corris Joy Train

...ergah, Photographer, Abergwynfolwn

Lluyngwern station in the early years of the century.

Hughes of Aberllefenni, 'asking for a reduction in the rates charged him for the conveyance of coal.' In his letter Hughes declared 'that in his opinion the reason for a higher charge being made in his case was that the Company's Manager was himself trading in coal. Mr. Dix had been communicated with for his remarks on the questions raised in the application.'

Matters from here on have a certain awful, inexorable quality about them: '23rd January 1907. The Secretary reported that the Manager, Mr. Dix, had replied on the question of coalfreight referred to in the letter of Mr. William Hughes, reported at the last meeting, but had not dealt with the suggestion that he himself was engaged in trading in coal. Mr. Dix had therefore been informed that the Directors had been under the impression that their Manager was wholly engaged on the Company's business, and was desired to state whether there was any foundation for the suggestion that he was trading as a coal merchant.'

In reply to this latter question Dix had stated that 'he had been and still was a shareholder in the Corris Coal Company, whereupon he was asked to supplement this information by informing the Directors who were the shareholders in this coal company, to what extent he himself was interested and how and where the business was carried on. To these further questions he had replied in a letter dated the 16th January, giving particulars of his interest in the Corris Coal Company.' Company.'

This was the end of Mr. Dix, though matters ground on; the Board searched out and decided upon a replacement in readiness for Dix's dismissal and the changeover was formally accomplished at a meeting on 28th May 1907....

Dismissal of Manager

It was resolved to dispense with the services of Mr. J.R.Dix, the Manager at Corris, and the Managing Director was requested to formally dismiss Mr. Dix and hand him a cheque for £50, being three month's salary in lieu of notice.

Appointment of new Manager

The Managing Director reported that Mr. J.J.O'Sullivan had applied for the position of Manager. Mr. O'Sullivan has had considerable experience as a railway manager, having been for the past 22 years General Manager of the Cork, Blackrock and Passage Railway, and after consideration it was Resolved that Mr. J.J.O'Sullivan be appointed Manager at a remuneration of £250 per annum.

Dix, doubtless embittered by all this, pressed various claims after his dismissal, which turns out to have been harsh. His days had, pretty obviously been 'numbered' in any event but the last references in the Corris Minutes, before they peter out in 1908, state that 'action is likely in January.' Dix's activities, apparently, were subsequently found to have had the earlier sanction of a less evilly-disposed Board but he was never reinstated, and died in 1928.

The first deficit in the accounts, ironically, comes in the year of Dix's fall, £63.14s.6d. 'carried forward to the next account.' Shortly after this the long period of documented meetings comes to an end.

O'sullivan (at a salary of £250 p.a. £50 more than Dix) came to the Corris as it tottered on the very edge so far as its finances were concerned; moreover it was embroiled in legal actions (apart from the aftermath of Dix there were problems with the Dovey bridge − see elsewhere) and his activities were necessarily restricted. A disastrous effort at Sunday services (coming from Ireland he should have known better?)

broke on the rock of Welsh Chapel and ideas of an electric powered extension to join up with the Talyllyn came to nought on grounds of cost. Returns were unremittingly gloomy. The company office at Corris station was abandoned and O'sullivan operated afterwards from the new Machynlleth station.

Horses and the difficulties associated with them − stabling in winter, what to do in frequent spells of lameness and so on, had much occupied Dix and one of the more successful 'new broom' efforts of O'sullivan concerned their replacement by the then very new motor coach. Cozens tells of O'sullivan's trip to Towyn, with high hopes in April 1908, to inspect such a vehicle only to be disappointed with its condition. It was 'unsuitable' and in any event required a new engine. The new General Manager was however undeterred, convinced of the utility of the new vehicles and of their economy over horses. In May 1908 Mr. R. Jones Pritchard (Cozens again relates) was sent to the Bristol HQ for his driving test and 'returned forthwith for the summer season to become the first Corris road motor driver.'

Business continued a decline, an unpleasant combination of traffic loss, falling returns and retrenchment in maintenance and upkeep. The Great War 1914-1918 naturally made for a drastic drop in the numbers of visitors. After 1918 the essentially Victorian tourist habit, 'taking in' such districts, never really regained the sort of popularity enjoyed at its height. Cozens records the drastic drop in passenger loadings, from nearly 64,000 in 1913 to less than 30,000 in the worst year of War, 1917. By 1921 something of a recovery had been effected, to 53,780.

Train mileage had been over 22,000 in 1912 and was only 16,639 in 1921.

O'sullivan died on 20th April 1917.

H.L. Hopwood travelled the line in 1919 and provides a valuable though brief contemporary account of its workings. He comments in *The Railway Magazine* on the Corris platforms for instance: they were 'all on the right hand side' and the carriages therefore required entrances on that side only. A similar practice apparently characterised the neighbouring Talyllyn though that company chose the left hand side. It is not thought that any political or spiritual importance attached to this ... There was certainly an optimistic air about the place after the Great War, whatever the true state of trade; several authors have suggested this though likely enough it was a country-wide feeling. The management had certainly 'done its best to encourage passenger traffic and vigorous policies had made the best of an unpromising situation.' Cheap tickets had long been a Corris institution, from the days of Dix (who was 'a firm believer in giving the public proper inducements to travel') and given the limitations and character of the line the numbers of passengers was considerable, even in 1919.

It was not really enough though, given the decline in slate. Hopwood rightly points to slate as the mainstay of the railways in the district and ascribes the decline to foreign competition. The importation of the blue-black rock was 'a state of affairs that should never have been allowed to exist,' a cry heard uncounted times in Britain since, but there was in 1919 a revival in many older home industries; Hopwood had every hope that this would extend to slate quarrying in Wales. 'And so bring renewed prosperity to the railways engaged in that traffic.

Optimism certainly did reign at that time and Cozens notes the *Montgomery County Times* of 28th Feb 1920, reporting the imminent reopening of a quarry at Esgairgeiliog ... 'other quarries are expected to reopen soon.' Timber during the Great War and its aftermath provided a useful traffic but denuded the valley of trees.

Machynlleth new station around 1914.

Corris, Upper Corris and Cader.

From the wooded intimacy of Ffridd the line came to the wholly bleaker (yet homely) hills, with their scattered and lifeless heaps of slate.

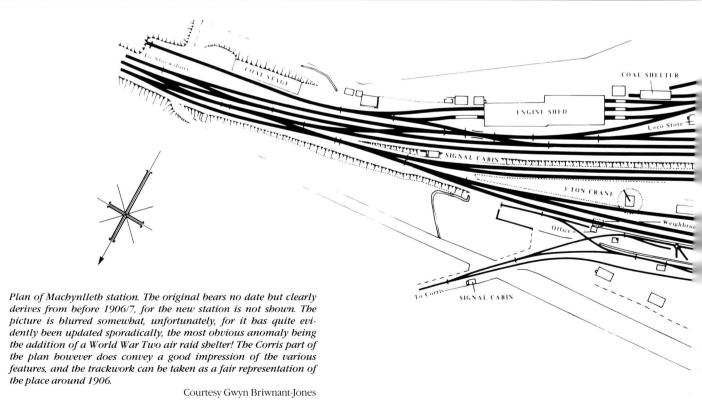

Plan of Machynlleth station. The original bears no date but clearly derives from before 1906/7, for the new station is not shown. The picture is blurred somewhat, unfortunately, for it has quite evidently been updated sporadically, the most obvious anomaly being the addition of a World War Two air raid shelter! The Corris part of the plan however does convey a good impression of the various features, and the trackwork can be taken as a fair representation of the place around 1906.

Courtesy Gwyn Briwnant-Jones

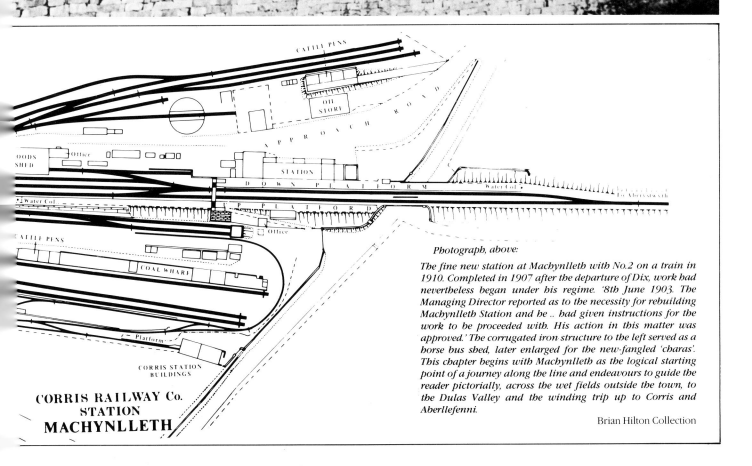

CATTLE PENS

OIL STORE

APPROACH ROAD

WOODS SHED

Office

STATION

DOWN PLATFORM

Water Col.

To Aberystwyth

Water Col.

UP PLATFORM

Office

CATTLE PENS

COAL WHARF

Platform

CORRIS STATION BUILDINGS

CORRIS RAILWAY Co.
STATION
MACHYNLLETH

Photograph, above:

The fine new station at Machynlleth with No.2 on a train in 1910. Completed in 1907 after the departure of Dix, work had nevertheless began under his regime. '8th June 1903. The Managing Director reported as to the necessity for rebuilding Machynlleth Station and he .. had given instructions for the work to be proceeded with. His action in this matter was approved.' The corrugated iron structure to the left served as a horse bus shed, later enlarged for the new-fangled 'charas'. This chapter begins with Machynlleth as the logical starting point of a journey along the line and endeavours to guide the reader pictorially, across the wet fields outside the town, to the Dulas Valley and the winding trip up to Corris and Aberllefenni.

Brian Hilton Collection

The original Machynlleth station in 1891, with No.1 on a train. 'The available balance of profit' for the year, to 31st December, amounted to £782.14s.5d, which enabled a dividend of no less than 5%. The year was also notable for a running battle with the Rate Assessment Committee and the death of a company horse 'from an accident whilst at grass'.

National Library of Wales

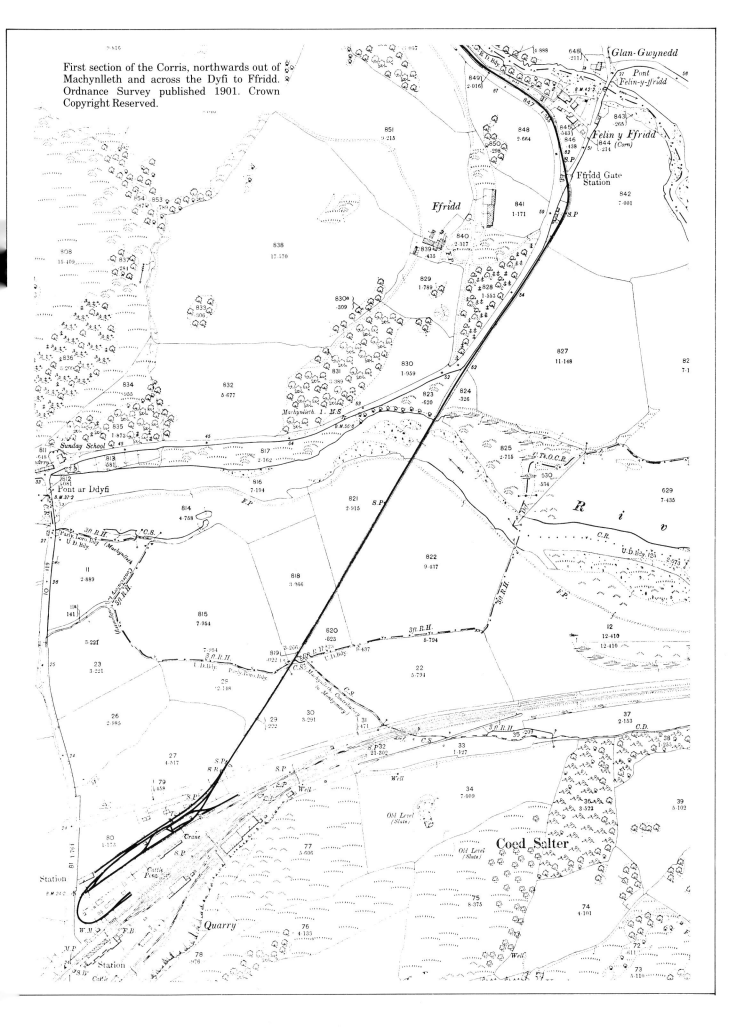

First section of the Corris, northwards out of
Machynlleth and across the Dyfi to Ffridd.
Ordnance Survey published 1901. Crown
Copyright Reserved.

The prospect upon leaving Machynlleth, 23rd August 1948.

H.C. Casserley

Brighter times. No.3 with two-plank box wagon and brake.

LGRP

An imperfect picture but one which, unusually, conveys an impression of speed on the Corris. Machynlleth in the 1900s.

Ken Nunn Collection, LCGB

The leaving of Machynlleth c.1938, showing ground frame cabin and surviving signals (most of them went in 1941); the hills in the haze beyond hide the Dulas and are a reminder of the climb ahead.

Lens of Sutton

The straight and level out of Machynlleth.

LGRP

Crossing the Afon Dyfi ('Dovey' in all accounts until recent times) on the old timber trestle, a familiar photograph, with most of the entire Corris 'moving parts' posed upon it. It is a postcard, once sold locally in Machynlleth ('the Corris Railway series') and the district, posted on 6th July 1910 to a second officer of the White Star line in Adelaide, Australia .. 'This is the toy railway that I spoke of ...' was the message.

Brian Hilton Collection

The Dyfi again. Like all the rivers in and around Snowdonia, it rushes off the hills very quickly and in the few miles of level ground left to it before the sea, is transformed, widening out to broad meanders. The enormous rainfall in the mountains and the steep slopes and relatively short distances involved means that the rivers are turned into boiling torrents with startling speed. Taking the pathway over the bridge as short cut could then be a risky venture. The pride of the directors when it was built, alongside the old timber bridge in 1906, erosion of the river bank here was to prove the line's final undoing. This first section out of Machynlleth was almost the only flat part of the line and was subject to frequent floods, though the footway proved useful in quieter conditions: 'a handy short cut for pedestrians venturing to trespass'.

43067. MACHYNLLETH: DOVEY RIVER & CORRIS BRIDGE.

The bridge in its broad valley, typical of the coastal rim of Snowdonia. Sir Clifton Robinson, Managing Director, reported on 19th October 1906 'on the progress of the reconstruction of the Dovey Bridge and anticipated that the work would be completed within the next two or three weeks'. It duly opened but nothing was ever simple on the Corris; there was a dispute and in the summer of 1908 Mr. Roberts, the contractor for the work, brought an action against the company 'in connection with his claim for £126, representing extra items outside the contract, for which the company repudiates liability. The action had been brought in the High Court and it had been ordered by the Master in Chambers that the claim should be heard before an arbitration. The hearing took place on the 9th July before Mr. Basil Mott, with the result that the arbitrator awarded Mr. Roberts the sum of £83 18s, together with the costs of the action. It was believed that there were good grounds for an appeal but in view of the comparatively small amount at stake it was not considered worth the Company's

Train bound for the Dulas. The Corris working instructions painstakingly put together by Dix and dutifully submitted to the Board of Trade in accordance with the law, provide a fascinating insight into the theoretical working of the line. How, on a daily basis, it corresponded to reality anyone can guess. Some instructions were laudable in the extreme, if over-general: 'It is of the greatest importance that all trains should work punctually to time, and it is expected that all interested will do their utmost to ensure it.'

Ffridd Gate crossing keepers house, the rough ground to the right marking the site of the station. The view is looking up the valley. Here the guard would solemnly dismount, unlock the gates and open them for the train. If the engine slipped, which was quite likely, the driver too would descend while the train moved to sand the rails in front of the engine, jumping back on as it proceeded past him. When rail conditions were particularly lousy the guard sat on the bufferbeam most of the way up, applying sand as necessary, from a tin can with spout.

LGRP

Flawed but unusual view of Ffridd Gate, as working station.

Chris Hawkins Collection

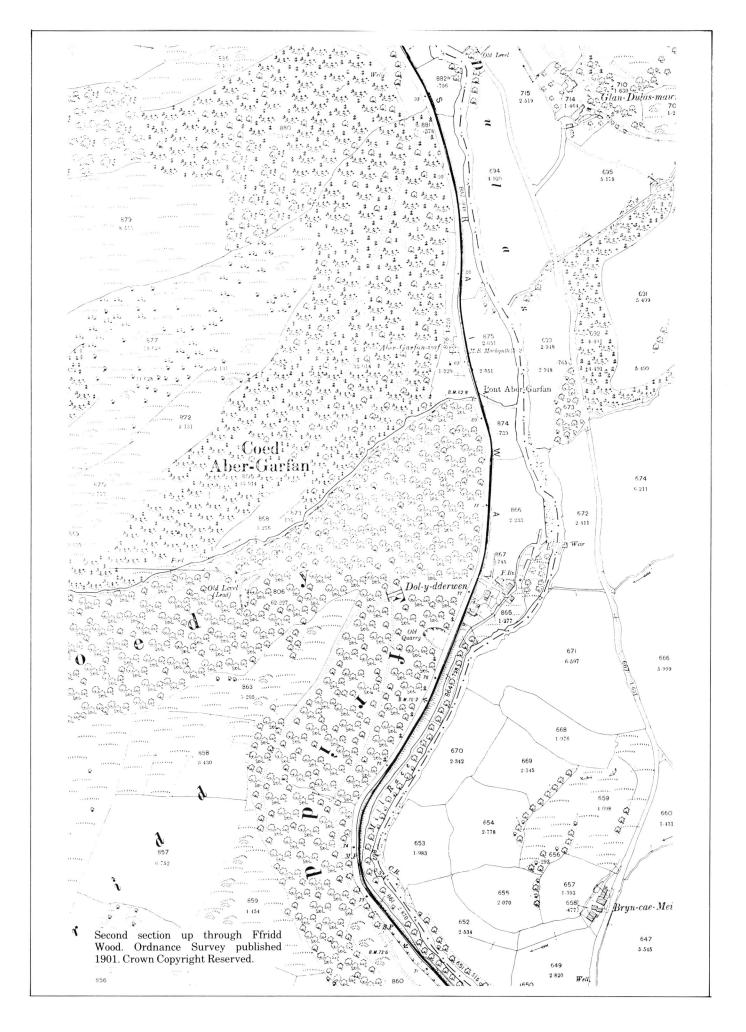

Second section up through Ffridd
Wood. Ordnance Survey published
1901. Crown Copyright Reserved.

FFRIDD WOOD, CORRIS RAILWAY, 4.A.

The classic Corris picture, Ffridd Wood. Household and all other writers have borne witness to its picturesque quality; the ideal setting for a 'toy train'… 'The valley of the Dulas is well wooded in its lower reaches and very beautiful, typical of mid-Wales indeed, the scenery quite justifies a journey on the railway. The passenger coaches are generously provided with glass – large panes along each side and end windows as well – so that every advantage may be taken of the views. It is a pity, however, that only the small centre windows at each end of the coaches will open, of more value for inter-carriage conversation than for ventilation! On a warm day with a full load of passengers the atmosphere in the carriage is not of the best!'.

Brian Hilton Collection

Ffridd Wood in 1946.

LGRP

Engine and van on the Ffridd Wood curve in 1946. The 'train' is going up to Corris, and the engines always 'pointed uphill'.
One is said to have returned from overhaul 'wrong way round' and did not perform nearly as well.

LGRP

Chapel and curve at Pant-perthog. Parochial and rural, vigilance was nevertheless required on the Corris – mist and rain could bring the train suddenly upon livestock, people, rockfalls or whatever and O'Sullivan, Dix's successor, ordered caution at all times. 1946: 'Trains must not be run through facing points at a greater speed than five miles an hour. Great caution must be observed in running over sharp curves.'

LGRP

Llwyngwern and train. O'Sullivan's instructions of 1910 continue; 'The staff are at all times to be prepared for the passing of Special Trains, which may be run without notice. Platelayers are cautioned to keep a good look out when using Trollies.'

Whellyn Collection

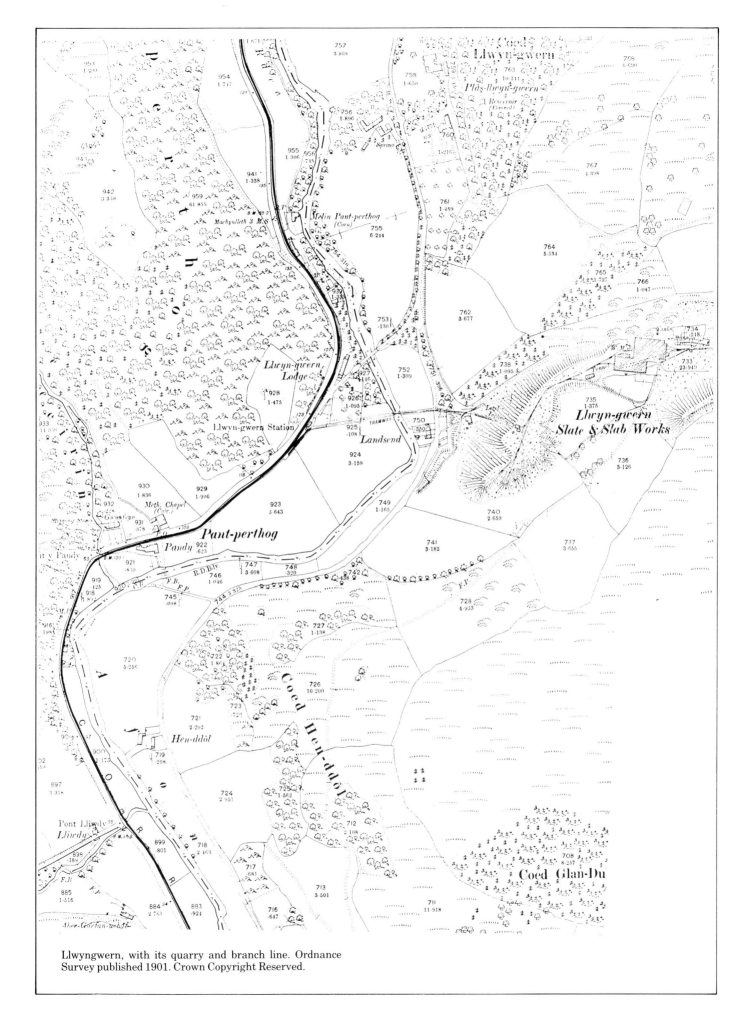

Llwyngwern, with its quarry and branch line. Ordnance
Survey published 1901. Crown Copyright Reserved.

Corris verisimilitude captured photographically at Pont Pant-pertbog (see opposite), 1946.

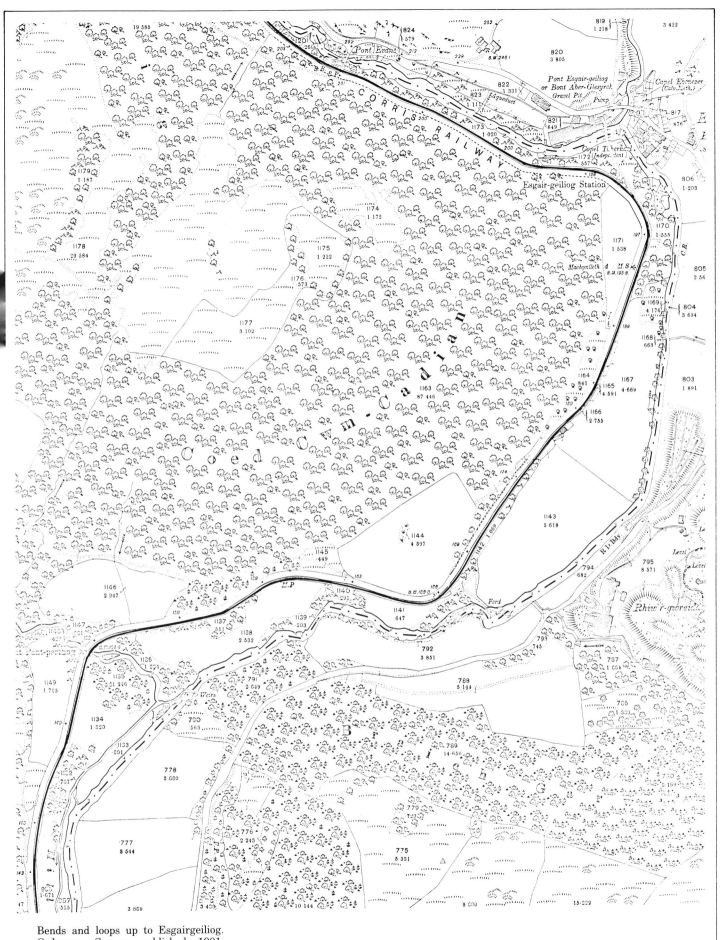

Bends and loops up to Esgairgeiliog.
Ordnance Survey published 1901.
Crown Copyright Reserved.

It is easy to appreciate how the Corris faded back into the turf after closure, for it crept unobtrusively along the valley side –
'of its progress there was scarcely a murmur'.

Both LGRP

Esgairgeiliog in 1900. This is the Corris in its heyday, with the fading years yet far off and its future, both as slate line and 'toy railway' still more or less assured. O'Sullivan again: 'Great care and vigilance must be observed by Engine Drivers and Guards in working down the inclines. Engine Drivers are strictly forbidden to make up for lost time. Every exertion must be made to ensure the punctual despatch of trains.'

Blasting progress in the Dulas. Doubtless, if the line had made it to preservation, foxgloves would have featured in the advertising: Household; 'Llwyngwern is the second station on the line, 2½ miles from Machynlleth, and from there for another mile to Esgairgeiliog station the route is very twisty and picturesque, trees on both sides, almost meeting overhead in places, with pretty glimpses of the stream below. Llwyngwern and Esgairgeiliog stations have just a platform and waiting room, similar to the station at Aberllefenni. None of the stations provide for trains to pass one another; a shuttle service works the line.'

Esgairgeiliog. A siding went off just south of here (see maps) and the Corris was pressed for payment 'for the use of Esgairgeiliog Bridge'. In August 1894 Dix was 'instructed to agree to Mr. Rowland's terms for the use of this bridge ...'.

LGRP

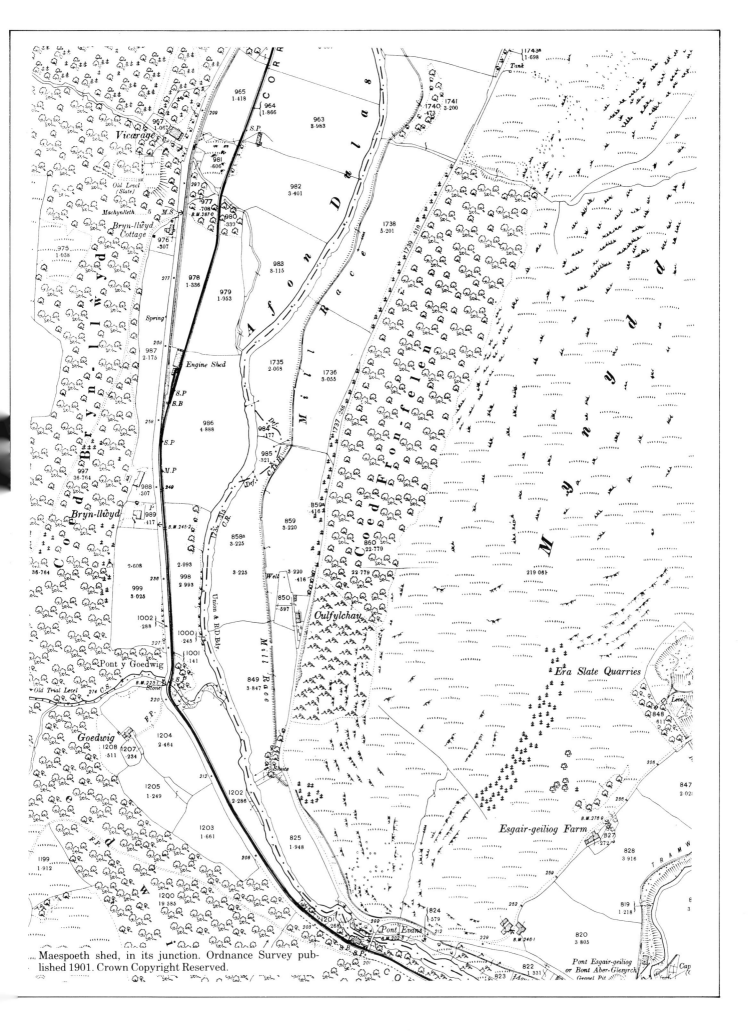

Maespoeth shed, in its junction. Ordnance Survey published 1901. Crown Copyright Reserved.

Pont Evans Bridge. Level crossings were always a source of particular concern, with most of the gates demolished at one time or another. 'At all level Crossings the speed of trains must be so regulated that they can be stopped by the hand-brake. This also applies to terminal Stations.'

LGRP

Approaching Maespoeth. Household: 'a mile beyond Esgairgeiliog, Maespoeth Junction is reached. This is the junction for the branch line serving the Upper Corris slate quarries and here the locomotive sheds are situated. The trains stop alongside the sheds for the locomotive to take coal and water.' Deriving doubtless from Dix's scrupulous overseeing of the line and its operations, (and an eye to legal liabilities – farmers and landowners pursued eagerly any 'loss') the Corris in contrast to its insignificance in terms of loadings was wholly dominated by fencing. When not confined in close slate-built 'cuttings' it was invested by the ragged fencing of slate 'posts'. If nothing else it demonstrated the easy availability of the rock in the district.

LGRP

Busy times at Maespoeth.

LGRP

The Maespoeth ground frame. Given the real nature of working on the Corris, an extract from O'Sullivan's rules of 1910 is worthy of note: 'In the event of an engine or train breaking down between two staff stations, the fireman is to take the train staff to the staff station in the direction whence assistance is expected, that the staff may be at that station on the arrival of an engine. Should the engine that fails be in possession of a train ticket instead of a staff, assistance can only come from the station at which the train staff has been left. The fireman is to accompany the assistant engine to the place where he left his own engine.'

LGRP

No.4 in 1924. Household, after his visit to the line, commented thus on the locomotive fleet in 1926: The Company have three locomotives in their possession. One only is now in daily use, as the other two are being reconstructed. Nos. 1 and 2 were built by the Falcon Engine Company in 1878 [see earlier Higgins comments regarding confusion over this, page 1] and have the following dimensions:- Heating surface, 170 sq. ft.; working pressure 160 lb per sq. in.; cylinders, 7in diameter by 12in stroke; driving wheels 2ft 6in diameter. The third locomotive is named 'Tattoo' and was built by Kerr, Stuart & Company in 1920. This locomotive has 109 sq. ft. of heating surface, but in other respects its dimensions are the same as those of the other two locomotives. Eight coaching vehicles and twenty-nine goods vehicles complete the stock.'

Real Photographs, Ian Allan

No.3 inside the commodious Maespoeth shops around 1938. This building really served as the works, with carriages dealt with in a wooden shed outside. Maespoeth was self contained to a fault, almost – the slate water tank stood inside and baskets of coal were passed out of a window *to replenish engines stopped with trains, on the main line outside. Engines took water at the same time, as passengers waited in the carriages. The staff, a fitter, a smith and so on were got rid of by the GWR.*

Lens of Sutton

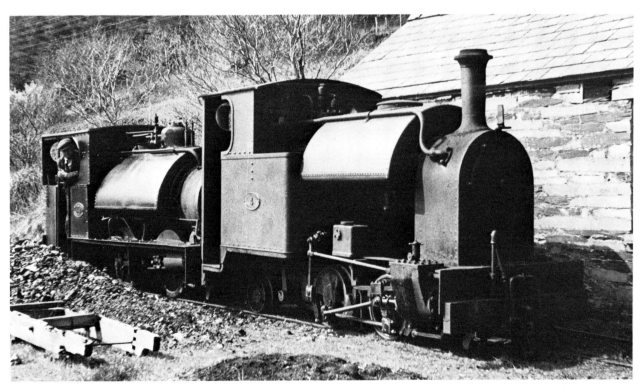

The Corris engine complement.

LGRP

Signal surviving at Maespoeth. O'Sullivan in 1910: The Danger Signal must be kept exhibited at all the Fixed Signals at Staff Stations except when it is necessary to lower or turn them off for a train to pass; and before any Signal is lowered or turned off, care must be taken to ascertain that the line is clear, and the regulations have been complied with. Working of Fixed Signals at Crossing Places: When trains which have to cross each other are approaching a staff station in opposite directions the Signals in both directions must be kept at Danger, and when the train which has to be first admitted into the station has been brought to a stand, the Home Signal applicable to such trains may be lowered to allow it to draw forward to the station, and after it has again come to a stand and the person in charge has seen that the line on which the other train will arrive is quite clear, the necessary signals for that train may also be lowered.'

Photomatic

Maespoeth with its ancient pile of ash and clinker, the sheep taking over, in 1948.

LGRP

Leaving Maespoeth, the half mile stretch to Corris. 1946.

LGRP

Train stealing through the bracken around 1946.

Chris Hawkins Collection

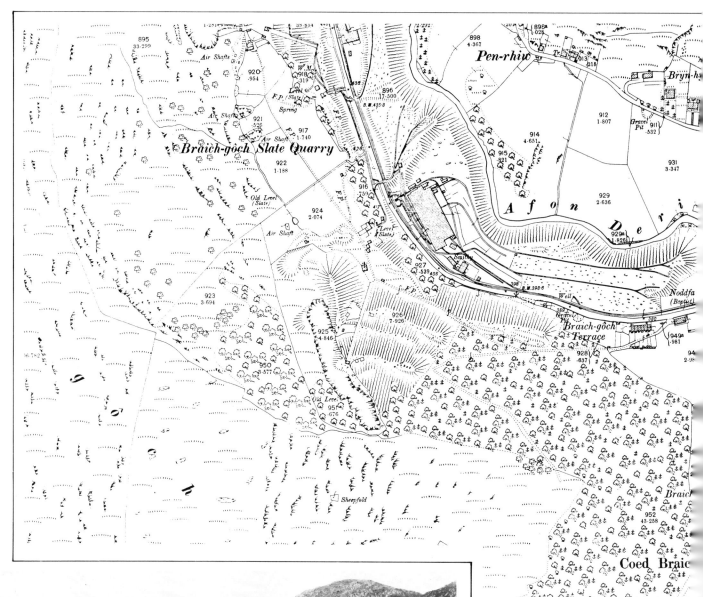

Braichgoch and Corris. Ordnance Survey published 1901. Crown Copyright Reserved.

Creeping slate debris at Upper Corris.

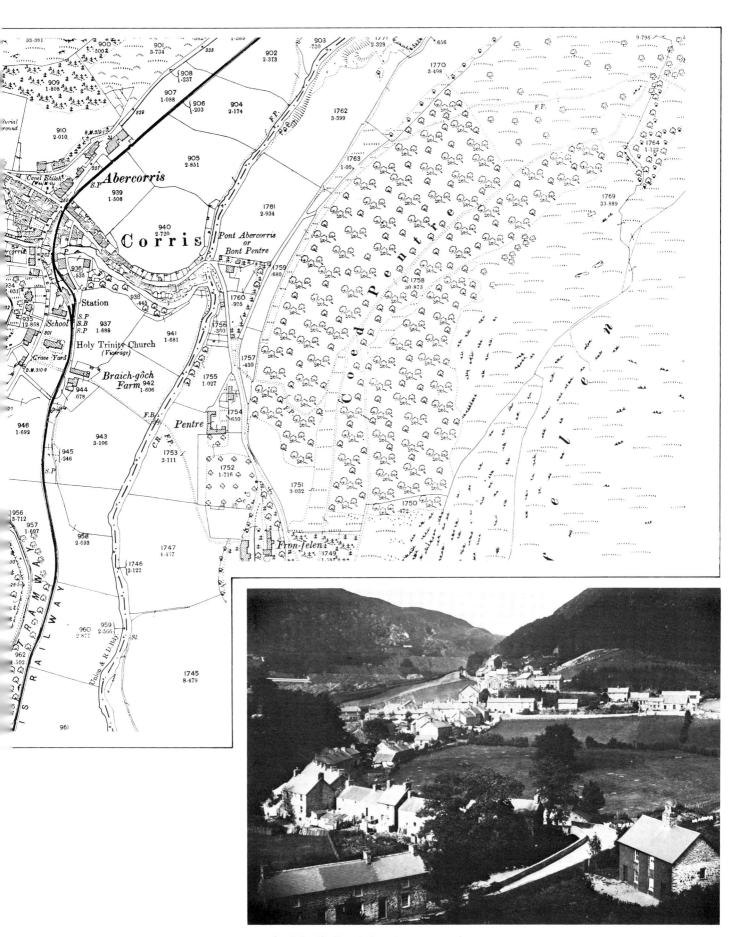

Corris itself, aligned along its narrow main street.

Corris around 1895. It marked the end of an operating section: 'The line will be divided into Two train Staff sections, viz: between Machynlleth and Corris which will be worked with staff and Telephone combined, and between Corris and Aberllefenni with staff only; trains crossing at Corris. No.1 Staff painted Red, between Machynlleth and Corris with Two Annette Keys attached, one for Llwyngwern Siding, one for Esgairgeiliog Siding, also the Key of the cabin at Maespoeth Junction which is to be kept locked and the signals not used. No.2 Staff, painted Green, between Corris and Aberllefenni with One Annette Key between Corris and Aberllefenni ... the buildings standing behind are cottages.

The Corris 'overall roof c. 1900s.

Hopwood Collection

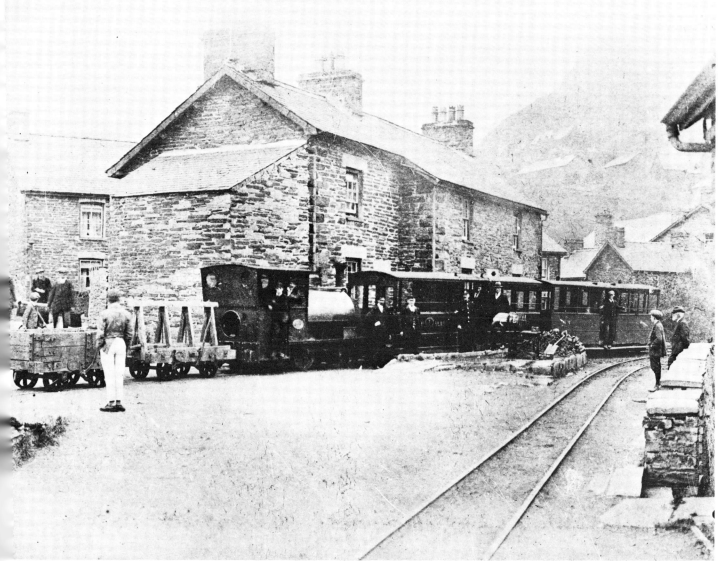

Corris around 1895. 'Passenger trains are to be made up as follows: Maximum for One Engine; four coaches and a van. The number of coaches to be decreased as the traffic gets light daily, and when possible one Coach only to be worked without the Van.'

Whellyn Collection

Corris about 1900, a view facing Machynlleth with the well-filled 'coal siding' (two 1-ton steel bodied wagons) on the left, by the Venus Soap advert. The Corris was littered with soap adverts, though what this said for life in the Dulas, or rather perhaps, Dix's efforts at generating advertising business, remains unclear. Trains seemed to begin and end at Corris with some frequency and O'Sullivan's strictures are worth a mention; 'Before starting from a terminus, or from any place where an attachment or detachment has been made, the guard must see that all the Automatic Brake couplings are properly connected; he must also look at the gauge in the rear van (when attached) and see that it registers not less than 18 inches of vacuum, before giving the signal to start the trains. If no van is attached both the driver and guard are to see that Vacuum Brakes are working on all the carriages, and the guard is to be provided with hand scotches. The Automatic Brake must not be used for stopping trains at Machynlleth and Aberllefeni Stations or at Corris when trains are timed to cross there (except in cases of emergency) and trains must approach these Stations at such speed as to be stopped by the hand brakes of Engine and Guard's Van (when attached). Care must be taken not to apply the Automatic Brake too suddenly, and when attaching or detaching vehicles to see that the Brake couplings are placed on the plugs provided for the purpose.'

National Railway of Wales

No.2 at Corris about 1910. Household's 1926 account: 'The station at Corris is quite a large building. It is provided with platform waiting room, booking office, etc. and is completely roofed in. The carriage shed alongside the station contains two tracks. The siding giving access to it is properly provided with catch points protecting the main track, as also is another siding which leads round the shed and runs on to the side of the street alongside the main track at the upper end of the station.'

Briwnant-Jones Collection

Corris in the mid 1890s.

Lens of Sutton

Staff at Corris: 'The street side above the station served conveniently as the point of tranship to rail of slate brought from neighbouring quarries by road, and also as the stopping place for one of the motor omnibus services operated by the railway company. There are relics of the pre-motor days here – partly dismantled horse-coach bodies lying forlornly by the side of the track. The company ran horse-drawn coaches before the present motor-buses were introduced.' It was desired to appoint the Corris in the best fashion that might be possible; Dix wrote in June 1892 that 'he had received notice to quit the stables at Corris at 12th May next and suggested that a piece of land adjoining the station be required for the purpose of adding a waiting room to the station and building a stable and coach house.' Consideration was 'deferred', for times were gloomy. Traffic had 'fallen off' and the slate trade 'continued depressed' but the passenger traffic showed a slight increase; 'the Circular Tour has not been largely patronised.' The County Council got wind of the proposal and presented 'A Memorial' in January 1893, 'as to the provision of Waiting Room Accommodation.' The Corris Board was unmoved (any local authority was regarded with suspicion) but the Board of Trade was also involved and on 29th June 1894 we hear: 'Further communications from the Board of Trade as to Waiting Room Accommodation at Corris Station were reported ... and instructions had been given to the Manager to negotiate for the small piece of land which would be necessary to carry out the improvement.'

G.M. Perkins

Glorious picture at Corris in 1941. Cozens was also in the Dulas that year; 'The station buildings here are quite considerable in extent and consist of the station with an allover roof, with a double roaded shed (formerly the carriage shed) alongside. The station further enjoys the dignity of a signal-box, low slatefaced platform and a run round loop.'

W.A. Camwell

'Beyond Corris' in 1946: 'the run is less interesting from a scenic point of view; the valley narrows and the country is wilder and not so beautiful. For a considerable part of the way to Aberllefeni the train runs between high stone walls set very close to the track and severely limiting the view.'

The Dulas scenery beyond Corris gave way to sheds and gardens, almost everything constructed in slate.

LGRP

Fields north of Corris.

LGRP

Garneddwen in the 1920s. The hut contains the ground frame; this northern section was signalled differently from the Corris – Machynlleth part which 'notwithstanding that the staff is to be indispensable, the telephone must be used between Machynlleth and Corris.'

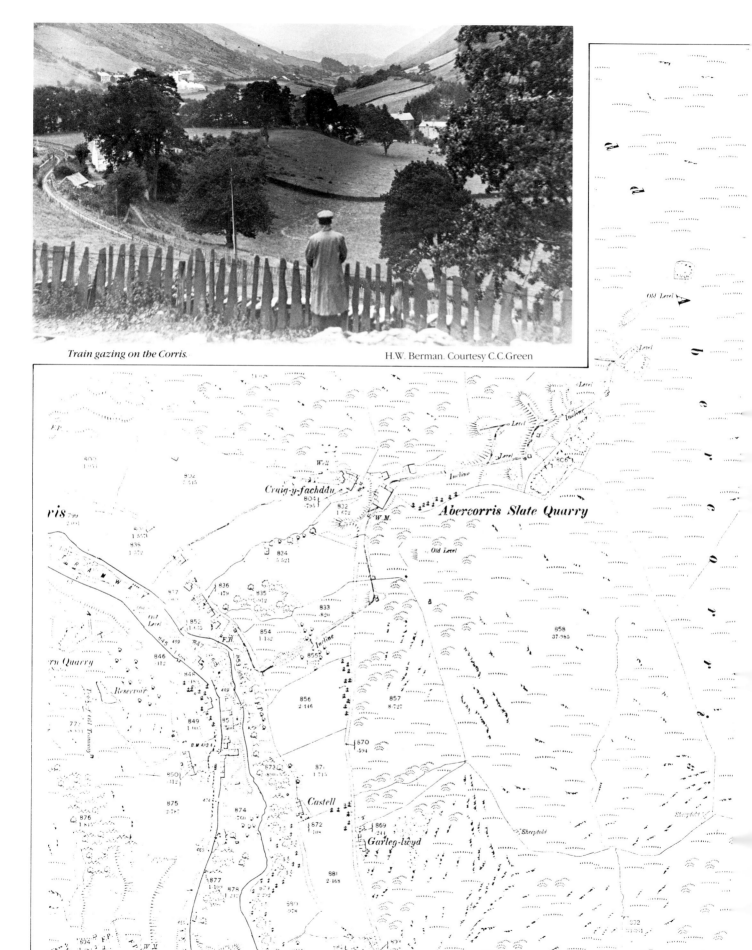

Train gazing on the Corris.

H.W. Berman. Courtesy C.C.Green

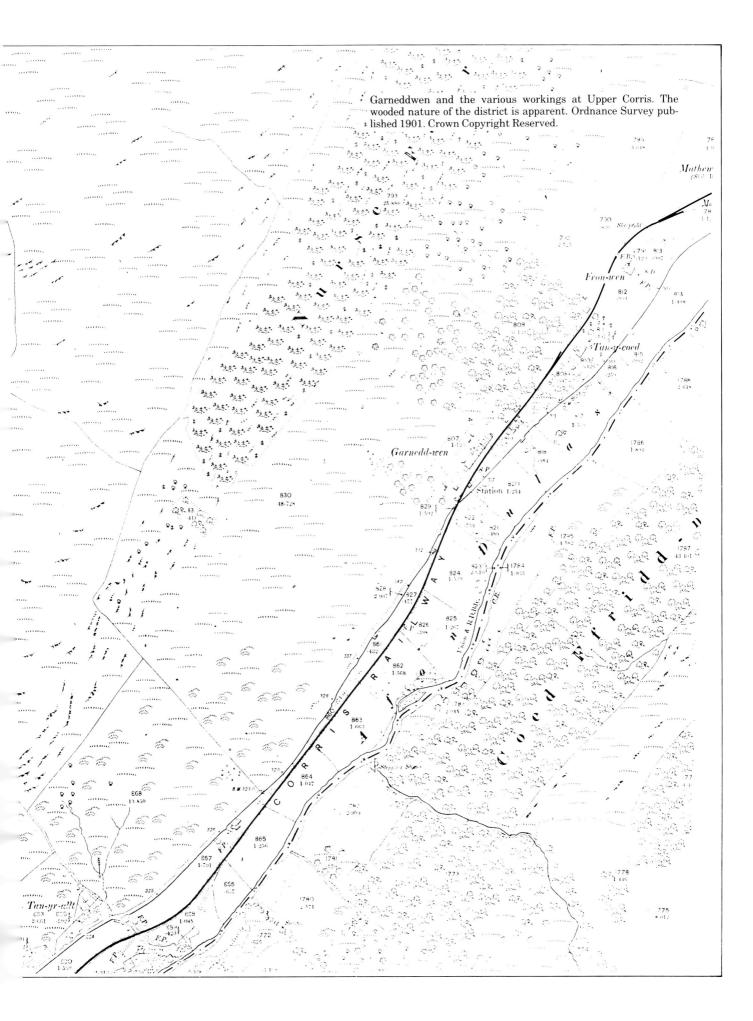

Garneddwen and the various workings at Upper Corris. The wooded nature of the district is apparent. Ordnance Survey published 1901. Crown Copyright Reserved.

Aberllefenni in 1946. Household's description twenty years earlier held now, if anything, even more truth: 'Aberllefenni seems on the edge of civilisation and the country road ends here as well as the railway proper, only lightly laid railway lines and cart tracks or foot paths lead to the quarries and farms in the district beyond.'

LGRP

Aberllefenni departure.

Aberllefenni, the limit of steam working, in 1941. Cozens reported on the place in Railways *the same year: 'Crossing the roadway on the level at Garneddwen station (six miles) we soon reach the end of our run at Aberllefenni station (6½ miles). This station has the usual waiting shed, and in addition a run round loop. The passenger train service shortly before suspension consisted of four through trains each way daily (excepting Sundays when there was no service) together with extra trains for part of the distance, or the full journey on certain days. The full journey time occupied 34-50 minutes. The signalling was of an antiquated semaphore type and would appear to have fallen into disuse. Locomotives are not allowed to work beyond a point a few yards to the North of Aberllefenni station. From this point the line becomes a mineral tramway and thrusts out branches to the local quarry and continues to the more remote Ratgoed quarry. The local quarry produces considerable traffic but the latter line appears to be little used.'*

W.A. Camwell

All station platforms were arranged on the same side of the track, as we have noted, and doors were thus provided only on one side of the carriages. Carriage seats were wooden slats, running lengthways ... 'a wide footboard and hand rail are provided along the door side of each car, and these enable the conductor-guard to pass along the train while in motion and issue tickets to passengers who join the train at intermediate stations. Locomotives and carriages are piped for the vacuum brake, but the brake is evidently not in use on the train as the flexible connections have been removed from the carriages.' The hole in the loco cab was for ease of firing.

Loco Publishing, Ian Allan

Aberllefenni in more businesslike mode in the 1920s. The Corris track was actually quite well laid, despite my earlier comments on an 'undignified progress'. Several writers have noted its steady gait, usually in terms of mild surprise. The signals were not removed until the Second World War, though they had fallen out of use before even Household's visit in 1926: 'The main line was at one time signalled for there are a number of semaphores to be seen, though they are not now in use. Some signal posts have single arms and some two arms mounted to point in opposite directions, T-shaped, one for up and one for down trains.'

Loco Publishing

W.A. Camwell

Standard slate load at Aberllefenni in 1941.

No.4 at Aberllefenni.

Loco Publishing, Ian Allan

Jinking and bouncing progress – No.3 making its way home from Aberllefenni, about 1946. Faces at the brake van window indicate an illicit lift for someone.

Lens of Sutton

Dying embers, Aberllefenni, 1946.

LGRP

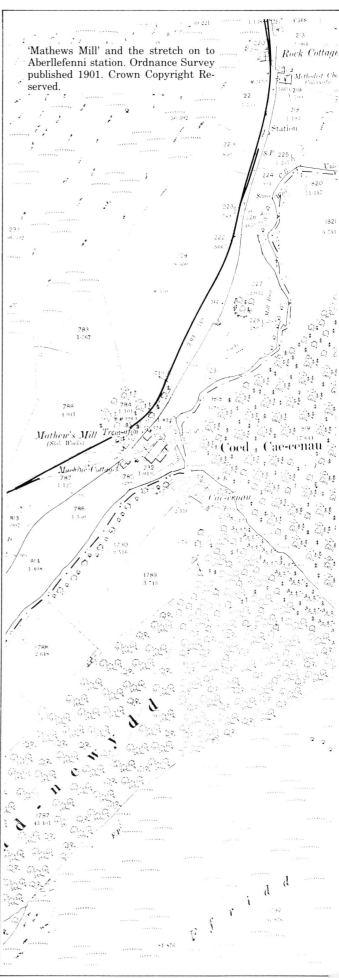

'Mathews Mill' and the stretch on to Aberllefenni station. Ordnance Survey published 1901. Crown Copyright Reserved.

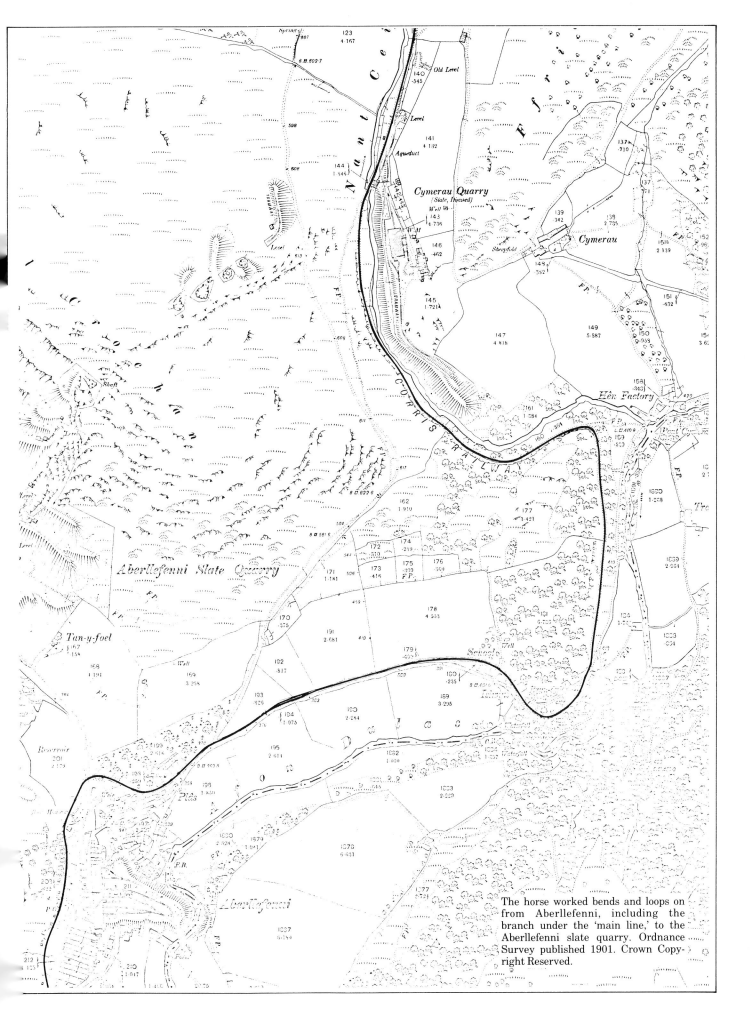

The horse worked bends and loops on from Aberllefenni, including the branch under the 'main line,' to the Aberllefenni slate quarry. Ordnance Survey published 1901. Crown Copyright Reserved.

Beyond Aberllefenni the line straggled out, groping its way to the Aberllefenni, Cymerau and Ratgoed quarries. Here it crosses the reservoir north of the village, around 1945. Loads were horse worked from here on though the full route has been highlighted on the accompanying O.S. plans.

LGRP

Despite the steam railway and the intricate politicking between the Dulas and far-off Bristol, slate production relied ultimately on the humble Dulas horse – bought second or third hand at some distant auction to serve out their days in the hauling of slate.

LGRP

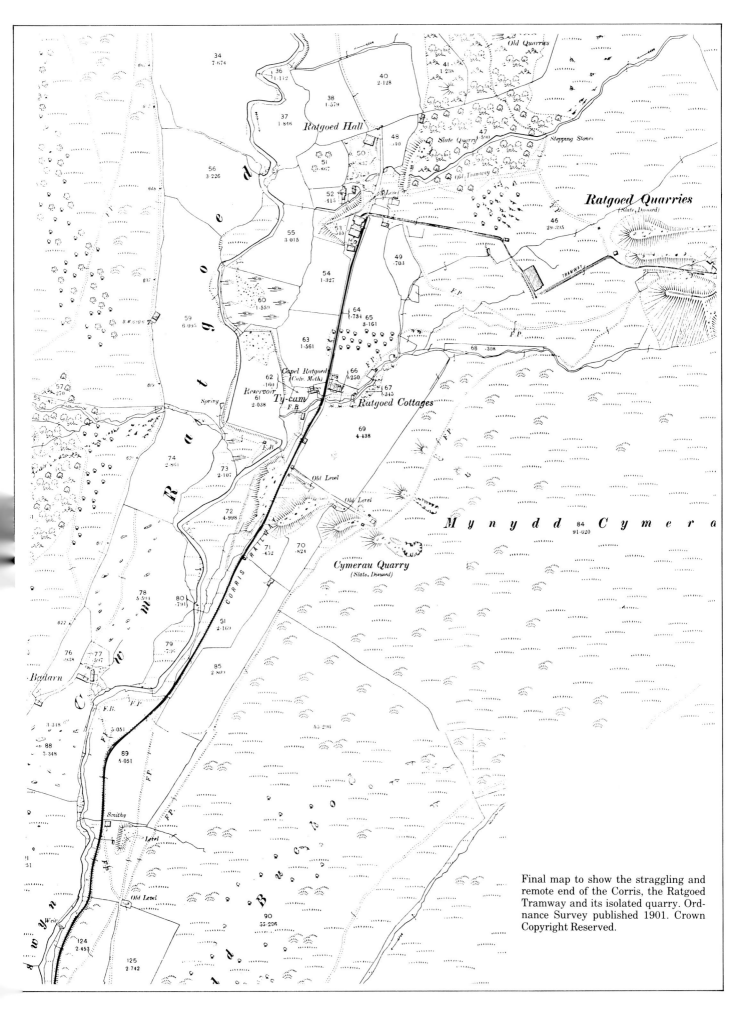

Final map to show the straggling and remote end of the Corris, the Ratgoed Tramway and its isolated quarry. Ordnance Survey published 1901. Crown Copyright Reserved.

Journeys end and nearly the end of the Corris, the straggling curves and corners of the Ratgoed in the late 1940s.

LGRP

Chapter Seven
Fading Away

Last but one train; Corris in early August 1948.

John Norris

The Corris passed to the Great Western in August 1930, finally in accordance with the aims of its directors, and at last gave up its passenger service on 1st January 1931. It was a bow to the inevitable and after the brief flash of post-war optimism the 1920s was not a happy decade. Bus competition proved too much, and only the Corris could find itself in competition with itself, operating bus services from Machynlleth to Aberdovey and Towyn, to Aberystwyth, Dinas Mawddwy, Dolgelley and Newtown. Added to this, there were Great Western buses to contend with, too.

Part of Bristol Tramways by 1923, the Corris had avoided, unlike the neighbouring Cambrian, the railway Grouping of that year. A complex re-ordering of ownership took place, the GWR buying up the Corris as 'job lot' to the more attractive bus services. At the same time Bristol Tramways were happy to get out of the area and all bus routes passed to the Wrexham Transport Company, the GWR having a financial stake.

Distant and lofty, the GWR authorities, having ended the passenger service could, after a rash of economies, leave the Corris to gently moulder in its hills, a sort of extended quarry siding. The loss of the passenger trains seemed to have been considered more or less inevitable locally and Cozens makes this point well, for in a perusal of the local press he was unable to find any reference to the end of passenger trains at all. It was obviously regarded as quite unremarkable. Engines 1 and 2 were scrapped and the coaches disposed of.

The GWR years were the years of the Corris Railway's dotage, though trains still ran on a daily basis in the 1930s, 'a daily goods service in each direction on weekdays, the time allowed for the six and a half mile journey being one hour exactly.' The locomotives, Cozens relates, took 25 minutes to run light from Maespoeth to Machynlleth for the commencement of the morning service, and at the day's finish the engine made its way again light from Machynlleth to the shed.

The line in the 1930s presented a strange, almost uncomfortable appearance. The train still made its dogged way up and down the valley but on a railway increasingly passing into dereliction. The vegetation, ground cover and lineside bushes, grew wilder by the season, luxuriating as only a wet sheltered Welsh valley can. The platforms crumbled, the various station buildings grew tatty, gates fell apart and signals leaned at crazy angles as the whole body of the railway began a slow passing into the earth. Dix would have wept.

In October 1943 the daily service was reduced still further to a simple trip on Mondays, Wednesdays and Fridays. The days were actually changed officially but the trains kept to the old ones anyway(!). The (Great) Western Region authorities seemed happy enough to let the line totter its way into the 1950s and it is a matter of enormous regret that the final demise came about in a strangely sudden (yet not wholly unforeseen) fashion, extinguishing the line before a nascent preservation movement could prove its salvation. With no Dix to act upon rockfalls or other hazards of nature the Dovey in the last years had encroached upon the trackbed. It was rushing against the very sleepers in the last months (the engine was even stabled at Machynlleth, lest it be marooned at Maespoeth by an untimely spate) and abandonment was finally forced on Monday 23rd August 1948; the last train had travelled the line on the previous Friday, August 20th 1948. Missing by a few years the chance of preservation, the opportunity for 'one of the most delightful trips to be found in the kingdom' had gone at last.

The final demise of the line was comprehensively noted in the railway press, in an age when any railway closure was at least a little unusual. In terms of general news, an account appeared in *The Liverpool Daily Post,* frequently an excellent source with respect to railway events, in contrast to many of our newspapers ... *24th August 1948 ... One of the most picturesque lines in North Wales – the Corris Railway, with its 2ft 3ins gauge of about six miles in length – was closed yesterday after eighty nine years of service to industry ... Mr. Campbell Thomas, station master at Machynlleth, told the Daily Post last night that the position had given rise to anxiety for some time ... The River Dovey had been in flood many times in past years, and the water had gradually eaten its way nearer the permanent way. 'Now the water has penetrated right under the sleepers,' he said. The service has been stopped, and it is not likely to be resumed.' ... It was in 1878 that the line began its career as a proper narrow gauge railway and because of its quaintness and the picturesque scenery, attracted considerable passenger traffic ...*

During the half year ending December 31st, 1897, tickets issued reached a total of 53,902 single fares and 18,920 weekly tickets. Workmen went to the quarries at Corris travelling thirty miles for '1s. In 1930 the railway was bought by the GWR and the following year passenger services were withdrawn. Gradually the line has been reduced to its present length.

Latterly the railway carried coal and general merchandise to Corris valley, and brought down slates and slabs from the quarries to be transferred to the main line at Machynlleth.

Standing silently in the sidings yesterday were the two small saddletank engines, and twelve small trucks . For forty years, sixty seven years old Mr. Pryce Owen, the guard, has been associated with the line and driver Humphrey Humphreys also has seen long service.

An Aside

It is a measure of the diligence and ingenuity of Dix that he was able to catapult the obscure Corris into the pages of the very new *Railway Magazine* of 1899. The article, by T.Booth, is fascinating not only for the historical detail but for its 'horse's mouth' quality. It was after all, essentially an interview with Dix and a portrait of him dominates the first page (he looked a bit like Leon Trotsky, a calamitous comparison all round, but one at which, it can be suspected, he might privately chuckle). Tourism within the British Isles was then prospering as never before (for the well-off) as the benefits of time and ease made their attractions felt. The middle class had arrived en masse and en famille. This was seen as the great saviour of such concerns as the Corris and certainly it liberated the marketing flair of Dix. 'Toy railways' was an important phrase and was used heavily in the promotion of the Corris and others. Booth's article mentions this at the outset, arguing that 'when the history of 'toy railways' comes to be written ... the CR will take an honoured place amongst them.' Booth drew attention to the flocking tourists, 'the increasing thousands who yearly visit the neighbourhood of the Corris ... and to those who are yet unacquainted with the picturesque treat which lies in store for them, our advice to such is not to neglect the opportunity of making one of the most delightful trips to be found in the kingdom.'

Booth amusingly and accurately describes the beginnings of the line; it was 'not of mushroom growth' but with the arrival of Dix things began to look up. The 'dry bones' of the company were shaken up in 1878, Booth declares, with the move to steam and re-ordering of the line. Booth is particularly good on the consequent travails with the quarry owners, information he was doubtless getting straight from Dix. 'There then followed one of the most absurd restrictions ever placed upon a railway company. No passengers must be carried!' is the quote from Dix. It was indeed 'the most incongruous position any company could be placed in.'

Booth quotes the quarry peoples' opposition: *the railway was intended for the conveyance of goods and merchandise and in reliance that it should be so used every facility was given for its construction. There was not then, neither is there now, any traffic in the district to justify the line being converted into a passenger line.*

This is something which presumably Dix kept in a locked drawer somewhere, to bring out and smile at occasionally. Dix listed the gradients out of Machynlleth for his guest, which have been quoted by most accounts since: 'the line is difficult to work as will be readily understood when it is stated that there are gradients of 1 in 32, 1 in 34, 1 in 43, 1 in 46, 1 in 56, and 1 in 59. All these ... are in the first 5 miles of railway from Machynlleth, and for the same distance there are no less than 116 curves of which 13 are under 3 chains radius, and 35 under 5 chains.'

Dix gave figures for the traffic which are of interest at a time when the line was regarded as flourishing. The largest number of passengers carried in a day was 1,466 and the largest number in a week 3,293. 'Considering the carrying capacity at command these are very respectable numbers; in fact, the greatest growth which has taken place in passenger traffic is one of the most pleasing features in connection with the railway.' Even in 1879, prohibited from carrying passengers, the Corris had managed by coach to take 4,632 people during August, September and October. Some of Dix's calculations shine through the narrative: worker's tickets allowed them 30 miles of travel for one shilling and school children for the same sum 50 miles, 'in six months time.' This was presumably the six months prior to the interview; Booth's article appeared in June 1899 and the figures refer to the half year ending December 31st 1898. 82,000 people were carried, some 56,000 of them visitors 'who use the line for pleasure only.' Dix compared this with the combined population of Machynlleth and Corris which did not exceed 4,000. He knew how to use figures... It was possible to demonstrate for instance the superiority of the Corris over the LNWR – the Dulas, Dix calculated, saw an average of 5·36 passengers per mile, compared to 3·23 on the LNW and 2·30 on the Cambrian.

The Railway Magazine interview was something of a coup, though no doubt Dix had made the principal approaches. In those days General Managers tended to the regal and deigned not to give interviews, rather they gave forth from on high, a situation the harried BR managers of today might just envy in their private moments. Dix's position was of course different; like his contemporary Conacher he lusted (rightly) for such exposure but the fledgling *Railway Magazine* was in turn grateful and suitably laudatory regarding the subject company. There are some intriguing links too. Dix was comparable to Charles Conacher (see elsewhere) in flair for publicity, out of all proportion to the (in)significance of the undertaking. In Conacher's case (after his time on the Cambrian), it was the Isle of Wight Central. Their interviews are remarkably similar, especially in the cheek with which favourable comparisons are drawn with the mighty LNWR. They (Dix and Conacher) of course knew each other, as we have seen, having clashed in a fairly mild way and they long enjoyed working links. The article then, is fascinating and required reading if you can get sight of a copy. Cozens of course wrote the first (and probably the most useful, for its contemporary feel alone) account of the Corris, publishing it himself in 1948. He would have known the circumstances of Dix's removal or some of it but he refers only to the GM's 'retirement', briefly (rather too briefly), in 1907. Such matters were not written about in the railway press, at least in those days.

End is nigh. Natural processes – the formation and exposure of slate – brought the Corris into being and natural processes – the wandering mischief of the Dyfi – brought an end to it. Ironically, after the track was removed, very little further erosion took place, hardly more than a few inches under where the sleepers would have been...

H.C. Casserley

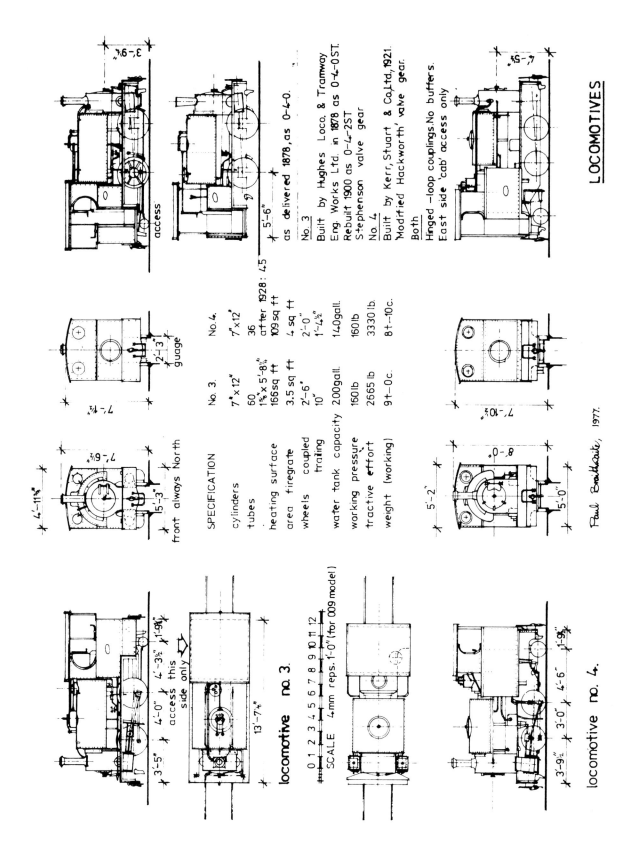

LOCOMOTIVES

access

3'-9¾"

5'-6"

as delivered 1878, as 0-4-0.

No. 3
Built by Hughes Loco. & Tramway
Eng. Works Ltd. in 1878 as 0-4-0ST.
Rebuilt 1900 as 0-4-2ST
Stephenson valve gear.

No. 4
Built by Kerr, Stuart & Co. Ltd, 1921.
Modified Hackworth' valve gear.

Both
Hinged –loop couplings. No buffers.
East side 'cab' access only

7'-4¾"

gauge

after 1928 : 45

SPECIFICATION	No. 3	No. 4.
cylinders	7"×12"	7"×12"
tubes	60	36
	1⅝"×5'-8¼"	
heating surface	166 sq ft	109 sq ft
area firegrate	3.5 sq ft	4 sq ft
wheels coupled	2'-6"	2'-0"
trailing	10"	1'-4½"
water tank capacity	200 gall.	140 gall.
working pressure	160 lb	160 lb
tractive effort	2665 lb	3330 lb.
weight (working)	9t-0c.	8t-10c.

2'-3"

7'-6¾"

4'-11¾"

5'-3"

front always North

Paul Braithwaite, 1977.

7'-10½"

8'-0"

5'-2"

5'-0"

locomotive no. 3.

4'-3½"

1'-6"

access this
side only

4'-0"

3'-5"

13'-7½"

0 1 2 3 4 5 6 7 8 9 10 11 12
SCALE   4mm reps. 1'-0" (for 009 model)

locomotive no. 4.

1'-9"

4'-6"

3'-0"

3'-9½"

Diagrams by Paul Braithwaite; drawn in 1977, based both on original drawings and on picture research conducted by Paul Braithwaite and John Scott Morgan.

Chapter Eight
Taking Stock

As we have heard, the line's first locomotives were a trio, ordered en bloc in the optimism of the late 1870s. They came from the Hughes Falcon Works at Loughborough, a firm well established in the specialism of contractor's locos; for that is how the Corris might, in its essentials, be regarded, as a rather exceptionally well kept contractors line. Nos.1, 2 and 3 were 0-4-0 saddletanks of simple, if not crude outline, some 10½ tons each in 'Indian Red' livery. Speed and climb were greater on the Corris than normally experienced in construction contract applications, and all three were soon converted to more stable 0-4-2s.

Shortly after 1, 2 and 3 had come, ten tram-like cars for passengers, each with four wheels arrived, to a street tramcar layout in fact, adapted for a lurching Welsh valley line. This indeed took its toll, and the 'wheel broke' on carriage No. 3 in 1887 'while running the 5.20pm up train on August 17th. The carriage however did not leave the rails and no damage was done.' The whole lot, with a brake van, was numbered 1 to 11.

The carriages were rebuilt in the 1890s to a bogie configuration 'to meet increasing traffic' and, according to Cozens, the bogies were designed by Dix himself. In this case he had undergone something of a conversion himself. The carriages had not been showing up well in traffic; Dix had been in communication with the Falcon Works at Loughborough in October 1887 'as to the cost of new frames for the cars' and reported to the Board that 'he was of the opinion that bogie cars would not be suitable.' The Corris was already on the lookout for new passenger vehicles and following a new specification a tender was received in November 1887 from the Falcon Works for two cars, at £145 each. A few days later a second tender arrived, from a company called Milnes, 'for two cars of tramway type to carry 12 passengers for £110 each.'

Despite the drastic difference in cost, usually a sure winner on the Corris, 'consideration was deferred.' On 1st December 1887 there was a further tender from Milnes, for a bogie car to carry 24 passengers, at £180 and (perhaps Dix was getting carried away with this tendering game) a leapfrogging one from the Falcon Works 'for a similar carriage to carry 30 passengers for £210.' The Board, canny to a fault, resolved that the Falcon Works be asked to quote for a 24 passenger car. Their effort was considered the best and the Falcon Manager, it was declared, would go to Corris 'to settle the dimensions of the new carriage ordered.' This was in the last days of 1887 and on 23rd February the following year the Board resolved that the new carriage (unlike the existing 'fleet,' in which entry was effected from sliding doors at end balconies) 'should be made without end platforms, having the entrance in the middle.' This would now seat either 30 passengers for £205, or 26 passengers at £195. The Corris naturally warmed to this arrangement, but not until the end of May did the company learn that buffers and drawgear were not included in the contract... Dix reckoned to supply them cheaper in any case, 'at £2 or £2 10s each.'

By now Dix was forming the notion of simply converting the rest of the stock to bogie operation. In June 1888 he obtained an estimate 'for an iron frame with bogies, to take ... [here was the ingenious bit] ... two existing car bodies at £57 each.' It was further estimated however 'that painting and the cost of transit would increase the cost to £80, or £40 per

carriage.' This effectively killed the idea for the time being but Dix, undeterred, pressed on. Adams, the sickly Reading fitter, was also consulted – whilst Dix favoured iron frames 'Adams was in favour of wood frames' and Ward and Gourley proposed to visit him and discuss the matter – he provided a sketch which was duly passed to Dix for his comments. Predictably, these were less than enthusiastic: 'It was difficult' he said, for 'Adam's sketch was not to scale and the price did not include wheels and undergear.' Any decision was deferred until the Directors could visit Corris again.

The new carriage at long last arrived at Machynlleth, on 18th August 1888, and was 'found to run very satisfactorily.' By September it 'continued to give entire satisfaction, passengers preferring it to the ordinary first class carriages.' The rest of the cars were afterwards converted to this arrangement; this was done at intervals over the years, for instance one frame was ordered from Falcon in October 1888, when it was also resolved that a second, new, bogie vehicle be purchased, 'similar to the last.' On April 4th 1889 the Board heard that 'the new bogie frame with two old carriage bodies fitted thereon had arrived and was a decided success. It was resolved that a second new carriage should not be ordered at present, but that two more of the old carriages 'should be mounted on a bogie frame.'

By April 1892 there is reference to 'two more of the old carriages ... converted ... into a bogie car ... completed in March.' The work had been done by Brush Electrical Engineering, and Dix was rapped over the knuckles, somewhat, the Board warning him that 'no further such work should be undertaken without their sanction.'

A summary, or the nearest anything in the Corris Minutes gets to a summary, appeared on 6th April 1893: *The Secretary reported with regard to the Rolling Stock that the Chairman and Managing Director had authorized the reconstruction of 2 single passenger coaches on a bogie frame, and also the alteration of one Engine and one Guard's van, and fitting of Automatic brakes to the whole of the vehicles named being put in hand forthwith; the Passenger Coaches were being rebuilt by the Brush Electrical Engineering Company of Falcon Works, at the price already arranged, and Mr Dix has already been over to Loughborough to settle as to the extra repairs necessary, the repairs and alterations to the locomotive being completed at Corris, the Manager having arranged to supplement his own staff with any assistance necessary to finish off that portion of the work.*

New coaches arrived at the end of the century, similar to the Falcon vehicles, built by the Metropolitan Carriage & Wagon Co.

The Corris owned one brake van, this was No. 11 in the carriage list but it was used on all types of service. It was rebuilt several times between the 1890s and the First World War, the result being a considerable variation in body planking and profile. The main fleet of goods vehicles consisted of company owned 1 ton steel bodied open wagons, and two loco coal opens of 1½ tons. Again steel bodied, the quarry companies owned over 100 slab and 2 plank box slate wagons, and also (before 1920) some conventional slate wagons. During the First World War some flat and bolster wagons were used on timber traffic.

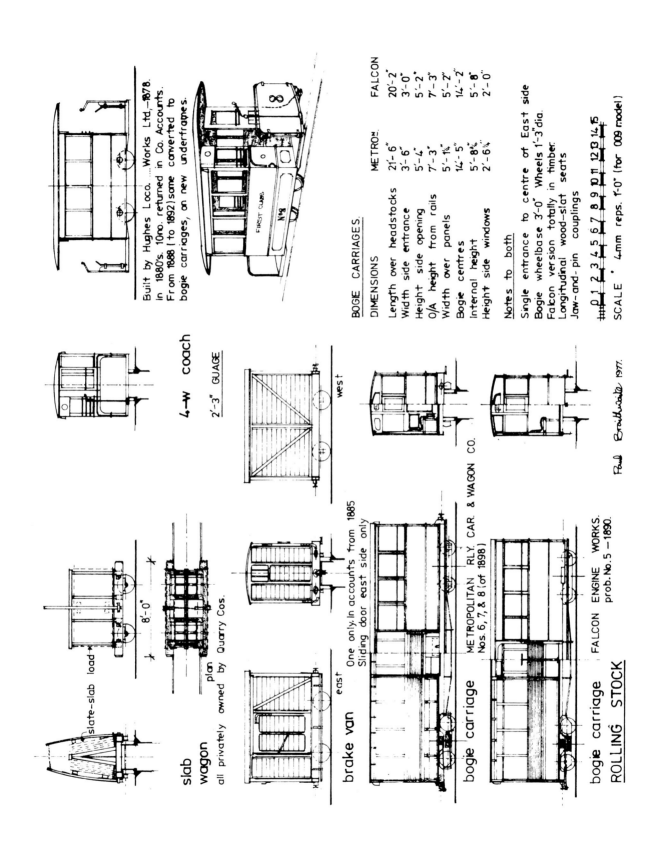

Built by Hughes Loco....Works Ltd,—1878.
In 1880's. 10no. returned in Co. Accounts.
From 1888 (to 1892) some converted to
bogie carriages, on new underframes.

FIRST CLASS   N°8

4-w coach

2'-3" GUAGE

slab
wagon
all privately owned by Quarry Cos.

slate-slab load

8'-0"

plan

brake van

east

west

One only. In accounts from 1885
Sliding door east side only

bogie carriage   METROPOLITAN RLY. CAR. & WAGON CO.
Nos. 6, 7, & 8 (of 1898)

bogie carriage   FALCON ENGINE WORKS.
prob. No. 5 —1890.

ROLLING STOCK

BOGIE CARRIAGES.

DIMENSIONS	METRO=	FALCON
Length over headstocks	21'-6"	20'-2"
Width side entrance	3'-6"	3'-0"
Height side opening	5'-4"	5'-2"
O/A height from rails	7'-3"	7'-3"
Width over panels	5'-1¼"	5'-2"
Bogie centres	14'-5"	14'-2"
Internal height	5'-8⅜"	5'-8"
Height side windows	2'-6¼"	2'-0"

Notes to both

Single entrance to centre of East side
Bogie wheelbase 3'-0" Wheels 1'-3"dia.
Falcon version totally in timber.
Longitudinal wood-slat seats
Jaw-and-pin couplings

0 1 2 3 4 5 6 7 8 9 10 11 12 13 14 15

SCALE ' 4mm reps. 1'-0" (for 009 model)

Paul Braithwaite 1977.